PENG[illegible]

# NAAM, NA[illegible]



Gp Capt. (Dr) Anurakshat Gupta is a general surgeon for the Indian Air Force (IAF) and has been associated with quizzing for over thirty years.

Flt Lt (Dr) Arnabh Sengupta is a medical officer in the IAF and is known to pack his bags often in pursuit of trivia and adventure.

Surg. Lt Cdr (Dr) Hitesh Mahato is a navy pathologist by day and a trivia-monger pretty much all the time.

Dr Anmol Dhawan is currently training in radiology and, when not looking at images of the human body, enjoys history, language and culture.

Sagnik Sarkar is a final-year MBBS student at AFMC, Pune, and their present quiz club secretary. Passionate about geopolitics and military history, he is known for channelling his inner Sun Tzu to deal with examiner ambushes in medical vivas.

35 INDIA

Celebrating 35 Years of
Penguin Random House India

## ADVANCE PRAISE FOR THE BOOK

'In India, books on the armed forces, by and large, get written for and read by the military community themselves. This quiz book, on the other hand, promises to be a bumper draw with wide circulation. The reason is simple: in a time of limited attention spans and multiple sensory inputs, it manages the impossible. Wrapping fascinating knowledge in bite-sized pieces, the book draws a wide arc from the colonial era to present times and holds the reader in thrall throughout. I commend it for the novelty of the theme and the wide canvas of content. The fact that it has been written by doctors, ace quizzers themselves, adds further to the X factor and makes this an unputdownable work. I daresay you will feel compelled to read it in one go and then come back again to chew it at leisure'—Cmde Srikant B. Kesnur, VSM, PhD, (retd), author and historian

'This little gem from 'Doc' Anurakshat and his colleagues is a beautiful compilation that has been put together with great care and passion. I am sure it will leave its readers amazed and greatly aware of the armed forces in India. My best to the entire team'—Jane Allen, managing director, International Quizzing Association, London

'This splendid book generously feeds both my passions: military history and quizzing. Most pleasingly, the text avoids the more typical staccato styling, the authors' Q&A being wrapped in rich and fascinating information, producing so much more than a run-of-the-mill quiz book. Gp Capt. Dr Gupta is to be warmly applauded for the result'—Chris Jones, founding editor, *Le Moniteur* (quarterly journal of the Napoleonic Association) and co-founder, International Quizzing Association

# NAAM NAMAK NISHAN

## THE ULTIMATE INDIAN ARMED FORCES QUIZ BOOK

ANURAKSHAT GUPTA | ARNABH SENGUPTA
HITESH MAHATO | ANMOL DHAWAN
SAGNIK SARKAR

PENGUIN
VEER
An imprint of Penguin Random House

PENGUIN VEER

USA | Canada | UK | Ireland | Australia
New Zealand | India | South Africa | China

Penguin Veer is part of the Penguin Random House group of companies whose addresses can be found at global.penguinrandomhouse.com

Published by Penguin Random House India Pvt. Ltd
4th Floor, Capital Tower 1, MG Road,
Gurugram 122 002, Haryana, India

Penguin Random House India

First published in Penguin Veer by Penguin Random House India 2023



10 9 8 7 6 5 4 3 2



ISBN 9780143462286

Typeset in Adobe Caslon Pro by MAP Systems, Bengaluru, India
Printed at Thomson Press India Ltd, New Delhi



www.penguin.co.in

MIX
Paper
FSC FSC® C010615

*We dedicate this book to all those who have donned the uniform and fought for naam, namak and nishan*

# Contents

# Foreword

Curiosity is not merely a survival trait. It contributes to engagement with the world at large, to growth and often to the joys of discovery and of making connections. Curiosity is what quizzers have in spadefuls, reading almost anything in sight, from jar labels to books across genres, often at most inappropriate times. Nothing is too trivial for them.

Quizzing is not as much about memory as it is about joining the dots . . . of working out answers from tenuous clues in the questions themselves, the change in the quizmaster's expression or from that occasional serendipitous leap of faith. The reward is that a-ha moment of undiluted joy, the glorious dopamine rush which leaves a silly grin plastered on the face for the rest of the evening when you crack that 'impossible' question that you ostensibly knew nothing about.

Parents and teachers sometimes promote quizzing as meaningful, scholarly jousting. But quizzers know that it is anything but. This wading through arcane trivia is rarely motivated by the desire to be productive. The occasional benefits, if any, are intangible and indirect; like being able to navigate a foreign destination much later in life. What it does though is to foster a lifelong love for factual accuracy, the skills of being able to rapidly cut through clutter and an attitude of being ever open to new ideas.

Indian military history, which is a source of much pride for those of us in uniform, is a subject that sparingly seems to interest our country at large. It encompasses tales of unexpected valour, of innovating to overcome insuperable odds, of mistakes, chaos and fun; not just of guts and glory. The pan-Indian footprint of the armed forces is something that binds us together as a people, as we chart our destiny as a nation.

Since our armed forces is a topic that is often neglected at quizzes, I am very glad that Group Captain Anurakshat Gupta and his team of ardent quizzers have worked hard to create this interesting resource. It is also a matter of great pride for me as they are all AFMC-ites, from my alma mater. As I read the book furrowing my brow, trying to recall some of the answers, I also chuckled at memories from my quizzing days. I learnt a lot. I wish all of them and this fascinating book much success, hoping that it is the first of many. I expect that the readers will enjoy reading it as I did.

With best wishes,

2 March 2023
Pune

Kaushik Chatterjee,
Surgeon Commodore, Professor
and Head of Department,
Department of Psychiatry,
Armed Forces Medical College

# Introduction

The authors are a group of doctors with one common thread running through all of them—the Armed Forces Medical College. Each of us started quizzing in school, winning laurels at various levels, but what changed our quizzing lives was the intense camaraderie and competitiveness that was a feature of the quiz club at AFMC. The spirited sessions of questions and answers, the intense mentoring by seniors in the club, the sheer madness of travelling to various parts of the country to participate in obscure competitions and the thrill of winning, is something that binds all of us. Three decades separate the senior-most contributor from the youngest one, but what is common is the child-like glee that one gets on discovering a new and amazing fact. The armed forces in India are shrouded in a veil for all those who have never served in it. The mystery surrounding the forces is compounded by the often inaccurate portrayal in media and the dense academic tone of the books that deal with them. This book is an attempt to address these extremes. We have tried to ensure that the content appeals to the layperson as much as to a quiz enthusiast or a military person. Jai Hind!

# Section 1

## The Colonial Era—Before the Beginning

If a list of people and organizations that have contributed to the birth, growth and current status of the Indian Armed Forces is compiled, many contenders can legitimately stake a claim. No single entity can be given the sole credit for what we see as the Indian Army, and indeed for the armed forces, as they are today. Some key contributors to this growth prior to Independence would include the three Presidency Armies of the British East India Company—Madras, Bengal and Bombay—the sappers and miners, the cavalry regiments, the sepoy regiments, naval powers of the era, maverick air enthusiasts, princes and maharajas, the European soldiers and mercenaries and so on. Each of them, in their own unique manner, helped advance the development of what is today one of the most formidable organizations in the world. There were amazing turns of events that often saw great men switching sides and aiding their erstwhile adversaries in times of crisis. On other occasions, international geopolitics dictated what happened in our subcontinent. A number of interesting facts and characters lie hidden from the general public, and we attempt in this section to present some of these. This is by no means an exhaustive set of questions, nor necessarily the most important ones in the entire field. However, in the available space, we have tried to give a glimpse of events, campaigns, terrain, people and historic actions that were, in great measure, responsible for laying the foundation of the armed forces of modern India.

**Q1. With a statue commemorating him at the Indian Naval Dockyard in Mumbai, which Maratha naval chief from Ratnagiri fought against the British, Dutch and Portuguese interests on the western coast of India?**

A1. Kanhoji Angre. The building housing the headquarters of the Indian Western Naval Command in Mumbai is called INS *Angre*, which lies in the same area as a fort he had previously built.

**Q2. A polar area diagram is a statistical tool typically used to plot cyclic phenomena, such as the number of births or deaths by month. Who devised this graphical tool in the 1850s while studying the deaths of soldiers in India?**

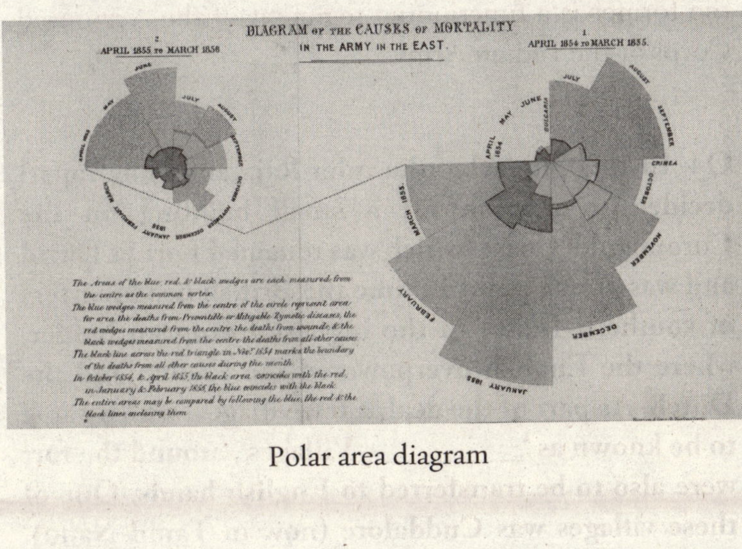


Polar area diagram

A2. Florence Nightingale, who had built upon her experiences in the Crimean War and applied them to overseas hospitals across the British Empire. The results of her recommendations made a deep impact on the health of troops all across the world and were instrumental in bringing down the mortality rates of soldiers in India.

**Q3. Which Anglo-Indian military adventurer raised two cavalry regiments in 1803 (of which one is still a part of the Indian Army today) and built what is today the oldest church in Delhi?**

A3. Col James Skinner. Of the two regiments he raised—1st Skinner's Horse and 3rd Skinner's Horse—the former is a functioning regiment of the Armoured Corps of the Indian Army.

**Q4. In 1690, the Maratha ruler Rajaram Chhatrapati decided to auction off a small building on the Coromandel Coast (which was renamed Fort St David and was at one point in time the British headquarters of southern India) to the highest European bidder, where the English overpowered the French and the Dutch. As part of the deal, a few villages, which came to be known as '__________ Villages', around the fort were also to be transferred to English hands. One of these villages was Cuddalore (now in Tamil Nadu).**

**How was it decided which villages were to pass off to the English? (Alternatively, fill in the blank.)**

A4. Cannonball Villages ('Gundu Gramam' in Tamil). A cannon was shot in all directions from the fort, and all the lands that fell within the distance of 'ye random shott of a piece of ordnance' (sic) were awarded to the English East India Company.

**Q5. The Treaty of Lahore, which marked the end of the Second Anglo-Sikh War in 1849, included the transfer of which entity (earlier annexed from Shah Shuja-ul-Mulk of Afghanistan) from the Maharaja of Lahore to the British crown?**

A5. The Kohinoor Diamond. The word comes from the Persian for 'Mountain of Light'. It is one of the largest cut diamonds in the world. The stone was mined from the Kollur Mine on the south bank of the Krishna River in Golconda during the period of the Kakatiya Dynasty and was initially placed in the Bhadrakali Temple in Warangal. Other notable finds from Kollur include Tavernier Blue (the Hope Diamond), Great Mogul, the Daria-i-Noor, the Orlov, the Nizam and the Dresden Green.

**Q6. Set up in 1887 by Maj. Gen. Charles MacGregor (an officer anxious about Russian troop developments in Afghanistan, fearing a Russian invasion of British India), this was reputed to be the first-ever department**

**of its kind in the world. Still a part of the Government of India, which department is this?**

A6. The Intelligence Bureau. The Intelligence Bureau of the Government of India was reputed to be the first-ever intelligence organization in the world, set up in 1887 during the period of the 'Great Game' with the intention of monitoring Russian activities in and around Afghanistan for fear of a Russian invasion of India.

**Q7. The Battle of Maiwand in 1880 was one of the principal battles of the Second Anglo-Afghan War. It was in this battle that Surgeon-Major Alexander Francis Preston, the regimental medical officer of the 66th Berkshire Regiment, was wounded by a bullet and subsequently sent back to England. Which fictional character did his story inspire?**

A7. Capt. James Watson, Sherlock Holmes's assistant and the narrator of most of the adventures. Some speculate that Arthur Conan Doyle created Dr Watson as an alter ego of himself as he was unable to serve in the army due to medical issues.

**Q8. The town of Wellington, Tamil Nadu, as well as the capital of New Zealand, were named after Arthur Wellesley (also known as the Duke of Wellington), most famous for having defeated Napoleon Bonaparte at the Battle of Waterloo. He also led several military**

**campaigns in India, the best known of which led to the defeat of a famous ruler in 1799 and brought an empire to its end. Who was this famous ruler?**

A8. Tipu Sultan. Arthur Wellesley defeated the forces of Tipu Sultan in 1799 at Srirangapatnam in the Fourth Anglo-Mysore War. He subsequently set up a cantonment at this location that lasted only ten years because many of his troops succumbed to malaria, which resulted in the cantonment being shifted to a new location—Bangalore.

**Q9. In 1846, two British lieutenants, Lumsden and Hodson, were assigned the task of raising Indian recruits at Peshawar for frontier service against Afghan tribals. A tactic used by the Afghan tribals in war inspired Lumsden and Hodson to introduce something for the local recruits. What did Lumsden and Hodson introduce to their army, which is still seen extensively in India and a number of other countries today?**

A9. Khaki uniforms, still worn by the police force in India. These uniforms provided good camouflage and were more suitable for the weather conditions. In addition, they did not require too much effort to maintain. These were also subsequently used by the British Armed Forces for their colonial campaigns and by the US Army, Navy and Marines, starting with the Spanish-American War of 1898.

**Q10. Severndroog Castle in Greenwich, London, has served as an important location for numerous geographic surveys and was also used as a lookout point during both world wars. Built in 1784 to commemorate Cmde William Jones of the East India Company Navy, victory in which naval battle led by him was the castle dedicated to?**

A10. The Battle of Suvarnadurg—which was anglicized to Severndoorg. Literally meaning 'Golden Fort', this fort is located between Mumbai and Goa on a small island in the Arabian Sea. The Maratha Angrias controlled and strengthened the fort and also had a shipbuilding yard here, which helped them secure the Konkan coast against attacks by the British, Dutch, French and Portuguese companies for many decades.

**Did You Know?**

The Indian Navy communicated in Russian to fox Pakistani eavesdroppers during Operation Trident in 1971.

**Q11. Which naval battle took place in November 1612 off the coast of southern Gujarat in which the English East India Company decisively defeated Portuguese ships, marking the beginning of its ascent in India? This is believed by some to have been the beginning of the modern Indian Navy.**

A11. The Battle of Suvali (Swally). It took place on 29–30 November 1612 off the coast of Suvali (anglicized to Swally), a village near the city of Surat. It marked the victory of four English East India Company galleons over four Portuguese galleons and twenty-six barques (rowing vessels with no armament).

**Q12. Part of the Tirah Campaign and the subject of a 2019 film, which battle does the 4th Battalion of the Sikh Regiment of the Indian Army commemorate every year on 12 September, remembering twenty-one soldiers who refused to surrender and were wiped out in a last stand?**

A12. The Battle of Saragarhi. This was a last-stand battle fought between the British presence in India and Afghan tribesmen. On 12 September 1897, several thousand Afghan tribesmen attacked a British outpost in Saragarhi. Twenty-one Sikh soldiers were present at the outpost who, under the leadership of Havildar Ishar Singh, refused to surrender and were eventually wiped out in a last stand after a long and bloody battle. The post was subsequently recaptured after two days by another British Indian contingent. All twenty-one soldiers involved in the battle were posthumously awarded the Indian Order of Merit, the highest gallantry award an Indian soldier could be awarded. The 4th Battalion of the Sikh Regiment of the Indian Army commemorates

12 September every year as 'Saragarhi Day'. The Hindi film *Kesari* was based on this battle.

**Q13. Starting with John Tytler in 1858, this list of thirteen men includes names such as Donald Macintyre, George Channer, John Cook and Richard Ridgeway. The last entry of its kind is that of Frank Blaker in 1944. These are British army men who were awarded the Victoria Cross (VC) while serving with which famous brigade of the British Indian Army? There are a total of twenty-six recipients of the VC in this brigade.**

A13. The Brigade of Gurkhas. The other thirteen recipients were native Gurkhas. Only British officers could be awarded the VC up until the beginning of the First World War. Many Gurkhas were given the Indian Order of Merit prior to this for amazing acts of valour.

**Q14. Stringer Lawrence came to India around 1748 and is often called the 'Father of the Indian Army'. He helped train and organize the Madras Presidency Army and laid the foundation for what eventually became the Indian Army. His benefactor was the Governor of Madras. Who was this governor, whose name is celebrated by a stretch of water close to the location where these two lived in India?**

A14. Sir Robert Palk. The Palk Straits and the Palk Bay between India and Sri Lanka are named after him. Stringer was the first commander-in-chief of Fort William and the East India Company erected a monument to him at Westminster Abbey.

**Q15. In 1465, Rao Bika led a force of 300 sowars or camel riders to conquer neighbouring territories. Ganga Singh led the Ganga Risala when it fought in the Boxer Rebellion in China in 1900, in Somaliland in 1902–04 in a failed effort at defeating the Somali Uprising and in Egypt during World War I. At the Suez Canal in 1915, the corps routed the opposing Turkish forces in a camel cavalry charge. The corps fought in the Middle East in World War II, when it was supported by the camel-mounted Bijay Battery, which became a mule team battery. Which princely state of India did this fighting unit belong to?**

A15. Bikaner. After India's Independence, the Bikaner Camel Corps was merged with camel troops from Jaisalmer in 1951 to become the Ganga Jaisalmer Risala and joined The Grenadiers as the 13th Battalion. It took part in the action to foil Pakistani raiders during the Indo-Pakistan War of 1965. After 1975, all of the Indian Military Camel Corps, including the Ganga Jaisalmer Risala, were disbanded. It still survives as a part of the Border Security Force, though, retaining the name

Bikaner Camel Corps. While primarily employed for ceremonial purposes, it is one of the few camel cavalry units still retained by present-day armed forces.

**Q16. What is the popular name for the 1901 Chinese uprising in which Indian troops captured the Beijing Legation Quarter, which had been earlier besieged by the Qing dynasty and members of a militia trained in Chinese martial arts?**

A16. The Boxer Rebellion. Also known as the 'Yihetuan Movement', it was an uprising against foreign Christian colonial elements in China between 1899 and 1901. It was led by the Militia United in Righteousness (Yìhéquán), known as the Boxers in English because many of its members were proficient in Chinese martial arts, which at the time were referred to as 'Chinese boxing'.

**Q17. First introduced by Maj. C.G. Bruce, the Khud Race was a protest against the notion that soldiers of a certain regiment could not compete on equal terms with Punjabis, Sikhs and other 'martial' castes of the Indian Army. Consequently, this race helped establish a reputation for this regiment and also had the effect of improving military skills associated with hill work. Which regiment is this?**

A17. The Gorkha Regiment. A phenomenal athletic contest, the Khud Race established the reputation of the Gorkha people as being practically invincible while fighting on the hillside, and also aided their operations in the hills of the North-west Frontier.

**Q18. This gurudwara in Ferozepur, inaugurated in 1904, gets its name from what village near Kohat in modern-day Pakistan, commemorating an event that had taken place there seven years earlier?**

Saragarhi Memorial, Ferozepur

A18. Saragarhi Gurudwara, named after the village of Saragarhi—the site of a last-stand battle in 1897 between Afghan tribesmen and Sikh soldiers of the British Indian Army.

**Q19. Udaigiri Fort in Kanyakumari, rebuilt in the 1740s by Marthanda Varma, the king of Travancore,**

**was also known as Dillanai Kotai, as its construction was overseen by Eustachius de Lannoy, a Dutch naval officer who, after having lost to the forces of Marthanda Varma in battle, was made a commander in the Travancore army. His tomb lies within Udaigiri Fort. In which battle did his forces lose to those of Marthanda Varma—a battle which perhaps marked the end of Dutch colonial ambitions in India?**

A19. The Battle of Colachel. This battle was fought in August 1741, in which the forces of King Marthanda Varma of Travancore defeated those of the Dutch. A consequence of this battle was that the highly profitable black pepper trade dominated by the Dutch was taken over by Travancore.

**Q20. Sultan Said Khan was a central Asian ruler who died in Ladakh on his way back to Central Asia after an invasion of Kashmir and Ladakh. The area where he is likely to have died is named ___ ___ ___, which in Chagatai translates to 'the spot where the great rich man died'. Today, this place is the site of an important Indian military base in the Karakoram Range and boasts one of the highest airstrips in the world. Fill in the blanks.**

A20. Daulat Beg Oldi, located at a height of 16,100 feet. The Line of Actual Control (LAC) runs about 8 km to its east. It is said that the sultan died of the effects of high-altitude sickness. The sultan was the ruler of the

Yarkand Khanate and was a descendant of Chagatai Khan. India maintained a consulate in Kashgar till 1950, when the Chinese convinced us to shut it down.

**Did You Know?**

The Naval Anti-Torpedo Decoy system is named after Mareech, the shapeshifter from the Ramayana.

**Q21. Ghulam Rasool was a Ladakhi explorer and guide who, as per folklore, helped a British expedition team in the 1890s find their way out of a valley they were stuck in, giving his name to a particular river valley. Which river valley is this, which saw action in 1962 and 2020?**

A21. Galwan River Valley. The river originates near Samzungling and flows west to join the Shyok River, which itself is a tributary of the Indus River. This is one of the rare instances where a major geographical feature is named after a native explorer. The web series *1962: The War in the Hills* is inspired by events that occurred in this valley in 1962.

**Q22. At the end of a battle fought in Europe in 1815, the victorious Allied Forces led by Britain sat down to decide where to exile the commander of the losing side. One suggestion offered was that he could be locked in at Fort St George in Madras, India. However, this was**

**ultimately rejected and a remote island in the middle of the Atlantic was chosen. Who was this commander on the losing side?**

A22. Napoleon Bonaparte. After his previous loss, he had been exiled to the island of Elba, from where he had escaped. A search was on for a secure location. The name of Madras was proposed by Arthur Wellesley, a former Governor of Madras. However, the proximity of a French colony in the form of Pondicherry resulted in this suggestion being dropped.

**Q23. The elephant on the logo of the Madras Regiment is a symbol of the Battle Honours given to the regiment for victory in which 1803 battle wherein the forces of the East India Company defeated the forces of Daulatrao Scindia of Gwalior and the Bhonsle Raja of Berar?**

Madras Regiment insignia

A23. The Battle of Assaye. Part of the Second Anglo-Maratha War, it was the first major victory for Maj. Gen. Arthur Wellesley and one that he later claimed was his finest accomplishment. He went on to defeat Napoleon at Waterloo but still counted this victory as being more significant in his military career.

**Q24. After the death of Queen Anne in 1713, the British throne passed to George I—also known as George of Hanover. His heraldry as the British monarch included the 'White Horse of Hanover'. This White Horse of Hanover can be seen even today in the heraldry of which highly decorated Indian Army regiment, with three Param Vir Chakra awardees in three different conflicts?**

Grenadiers insignia

A24. The Grenadiers. In existence since 1778, this infantry regiment was earlier part of the Bombay Presidency Army. It has distinguished itself in both world wars and subsequently earned Battle Honours like Gurais, Asal Uttar, Jarpal and Tololing/Tiger Hill in the post-Independence period.

**Q25. Benoît Leborgne was a French military adventurer who made his fortune in India. He became the general of an army of nearly one lakh soldiers, allowing a particular Indian statesman and ruler to dominate central and northern India in the late eighteenth century. Which Indian ruler was he in the service of?**

A25. Mahadji Sindhia or Mahadji Shinde—a Maratha statesman with his base at Gwalior. Leborgne was from the Duchy of Savoy and went on to become the president of the Mont-Blanc general council under Napoleon.

**Q26. The Panjdeh Incident in 1885 was an armed engagement between Russian forces and the Emir of Afghanistan. An alarmed British government saw it as a threat to their Indian possessions. Reinforcements were sent from India to defend against the threat. The effort was funded in large measure by the Nizam**

**of Hyderabad. How did this event affect the composition of the future Indian Army?**

A26. The establishment of the Imperial Service Troops. The British decided to create a reserve force of up to 20,000 men recruited from the armies of the Native States. The training cost and equipment would be funded by the native rulers, but the actual training would be done by the British Indian Army.

**Q27. The Chitral Expedition in 1895 was launched to relieve the Chitral Fort in Gilgit after a local coup. It became famous for the resolute fight put up by the 14th Sikhs and a large detachment of infantry from one of the Imperial Service Troops of an Indian state. Which state was this?**

A27. Kashmir. The 14th Sikhs came from Ferozepur while the larger contingent came from the state troops of the Maharaja of Kashmir. The entire episode saw the award of one Victoria Cross and eleven Distinguished Service Orders (DSOs). At least nine participants went on to become generals. The Sikhs were sent to China in 1900 to suppress the Boxer Rebellion. The VC was won by Surgeon-Major Harry Frederick Whitchurch of the Indian Medical Service. He later died of enteric fever and is buried in Dharamshala.

**Q28. The Boxer Rebellion was an occasion when many soldiers from the Imperial Service Troops were sent to counter the Chinese rebels. These included men from Alwar, Bikaner, Jodhpur and which other princely state from Punjab, which had been founded by an Afghan?**

A28. Malerkotla. The state was founded in 1657 by Bayazid Khan after he saved Aurangzeb's life during a tiger attack. The state joined India in 1948 as part of PEPSU—Patiala and East Punjab State Union—which eventually merged with Punjab in 1956. Other members of PEPSU were Patiala, Jind, Kapurthala, Nabha, Faridkot, Nalagarh and Kalsia.

**Q29. A Salute State was a princely state under the British Raj that had been granted a gun salute by the British crown. It denoted the importance and prestige of the state in the eyes of the crown. In December 1911, at the time of the Coronation Durbar, only three states were given the maximum twenty-one-gun salute. These were Mysore, Hyderabad and Baroda. However, two more were added, in 1917 and 1921, to take the tally up to five. Which were these two states?**

A29. Gwalior in 1917 and Kashmir in 1921. Both were upgraded as a result of the outstanding service of their soldiers in the First World War. Three others were authorized a twenty-one-gun salute within their own state but a nineteen-gun salute in the rest of India: Bhopal, Indore and Udaipur. In 1947, there were 118 such states—113 in India, four in Pakistan and one in Sikkim.

**Q30. Only four Salute States acceded to Pakistan after 1947. They had an entitlement of nineteen, seventeen, fifteen and eleven gun salutes, respectively. Which was this nineteen-gun salute state, which constitutes till date the largest territory of modern-day Pakistan? A controversial region by all accounts, it has been in the news for all the wrong reasons over the past few years.**

A30. Kalat. This is the region of Balochistan today. Interestingly, each of these four states had a ruler who carried a distinct title—Kalat had a ruler who was called the Khan, the ruler of Bahawalpur in Punjab was titled Nawab, the ruler of Khairpur in Sindh was the Mir while the ruler of Chitral in Khyber Pakhtunkhwa carried the title of Mehtar.

**Did You Know?**

An officers' lounge in the Delhi Cantonment is named after a mule. Pedongi, the celebrated mule, has even received citations for maintaining supply lines amid heavy fire.

**Q31. Although gun salutes were reserved for rulers and states, the crown made some exceptions for prominent people. These included one religious leader who had no territorial possessions at all. Who was this?**

A31. The Aga Khan, religious leader of the Nizari Ismaili branch of Islam, was entitled to a personal eleven-gun salute. The Dalai Lama of Tibet was given a nineteen-gun salute, but he was a religious leader who had a specific territorial attachment. The British also gave a thirteen-gun salute to the Raja of Vizianagram and an unusual four-gun salute to the Manyam Zamindar of Yanam, a French colony. Yanam finally joined India only in July 1963.

**Q32. The 1782 Treaty of Salbai made the British the virtual arbiters of peace in India, thus acknowledging their supremacy. It also recognized one princely state as an independent chief and not a vassal to the Maratha Peshwa, who was the most powerful leader in the country then. Which state was this?**

A32. Gwalior. Mahadji or Madhav Rao I agreed to withdraw to Ujjain while the Britishers agreed to stay north of the Yamuna river. This resulted in the gradual growth of Mahadji's power—to the extent that he even helped reinstate Mughal emperor Shah Alam II back on the throne in Delhi in 1785. Mahadji negotiated peace with Tipu in 1792 and helped establish Maratha supremacy over north India. However, at the peak of his powers, he died suddenly and mysteriously in 1794 at Wanowrie in Pune.

**Q33. Ruling from the age of ten, this ruler remained on the throne for over forty years. He visited China in 1900 during the Boxer Rebellion and gifted the British Indian Army a hospital ship for the wounded. Who was this able administrator of Gwalior and a well-respected colonial ruler?**

A33. Madhav Rao Scindia II. He was the son of Jayaji Rao, who himself had helped fund part of the Great Indian Peninsular Railway. Madhav Rao II was succeeded by Jivaji Rao, who acceded to India in 1948 along with twenty-five other princely states as an entity known as Madhya Bharat or Malwa Union. This union, with an area of over 1,20,000 sq. km, was merged into Madhya Pradesh in November 1956.

**Q34. The Scinde Horse was popularly known as the Scinde Irregular Horse. Why was this moniker used? And how was its role reflected in what was probably the most unique badge worn by any unit in the world?**

Scinde Horse badge

A34. The regiment was tasked with the protection of a vast region and thus, it often lay in ambush and travelled with caravans along this route. They dressed in civilian clothing to look inconspicuous and often raided the camps of the Baluchis to recover the loot. This led to the regiment being called the 'Irregulars'. The troops, however, had great respect for their adversaries and in their honour, they adopted a badge depicting a Baluchi warrior with his spear, charging on a stallion. It is thus the only regiment known to honour its enemy in this unique manner.

**Q35. Of Anglo-Indian parentage, this soldier served in the Maratha Army from the age of sixteen onwards. However, after the Second Anglo-Maratha War of 1803, he, along with all other Anglo-Indians, was dismissed from Maratha service. He eventually joined the Bengal Army and raised a cavalry unit called the 'Yellow Boys' because of the colour of their uniform. Fluent in Persian, he wrote several books, including an extensively illustrated manuscript called *Kitab-i Tashrih al-Aqvam* (History of the Origin and Distinguishing Marks of the Different Castes of India). Who was this enigmatic figure?**

A35. Col James Skinner. He raised two cavalry regiments at Hansi in Haryana known as the 1st Skinner's Horse and the 3rd Skinner's Horse, which are still part of the Indian Army. He became known as 'Sikander Sahib' later in life and in 1960, his great-great grandson, Lt Col Michael Skinner, took command of the Skinner's Horse—over 100 years after the founder's death.

**Q36. The first recorded use of artillery in India is at the Battle of Adoni in 1368. The Bahamani sultans used artillery effectively against the Raja of Vijayanagar. However, what raising on 28 September 1827 is commemorated as Gunners Day till date in India?**

A36. 5 (Bombay) Mountain Battery was raised as the 8th Company of the Golandaz Battalion of the Bombay

Foot Regiment on that day. It forms part of the 57 Field Regiment today. Though Babur, Tipu and Ranjit Singh all used artillery regularly, it was this raising that marked the formal adoption of this form of a fighting arm in the Indian Army.

**Q37. Pandit Nain Singh and his cousin Mani Singh were recruited by the British Army as part of an extraordinary project in 1861. The two trained in Dehradun for nearly two years for their expeditions, learning a number of surveying techniques. Because the survey needed to be clandestine, a number of innovations were used to hide the surveying. Mercury for thermometers was hidden in the bottom of a bowl, notes were stored inside a prayer wheel and survey gear was hidden inside the luggage. A string of prayer beads, which usually had 108 beads, was modified to have only 100 beads; the pundits were trained to move one bead every hundred paces to count their steps. They were also trained to have a precise stride length of 33 inches across varying terrain. What was this project that these men from Kumaon were an integral part of?**

A37. The Great Trigonometric Survey of India. Nain Singh reached Lhasa on 10 January 1866 and estimated the altitude of Lhasa as 3420 metres by boiling water; this was close to the actual value of 3540 metres. He also estimated the position of Lhasa with celestial observations. Next, he explored western Tibet in 1867, reaching the gold field at Thok Jalung, mapping the Sutlej River and performing an 850-mile-long route survey. His final expedition returned to Lhasa via a more northern route than his first expedition and ran from 1873 to 1875.

**Q38. The Trigonometric Survey of India, a project that aimed to survey the subcontinent precisely, was started under the leadership of William Lambton but was completed by his successor who later became synonymous with the Himalayas. Who was this gentleman?**

A38. George Everest. Assistant to William Lambton, he succeeded him as the superintendent of the survey. The project was instrumental in demarcating the borders of the subcontinent under British rule and involved precise calculations that also correctly determined the heights of Peak XV, K2 and Kanchenjunga, among others. Andrew Scott Waugh, Everest's protégé was instrumental in claiming that Peak XV was the tallest in the world and formally named it Mt Everest in 1865. The discovery was largely due to the calculations of Radhanath Sikdar, a 'computer' in the survey.

**Q39. The first was Kohat, the second Derajat, the third Peshawar, the fourth Hazara and the fifth Bombay. Well, Bombay was actually the oldest, but**

**still called the fifth. The first and second were raised from disbanded Sikh units following the Second Anglo-Sikh war of 1849. What were these?**

A39. Indian Mountain Artillery units, also known as Mountain Battery FF. The 3rd Battery served in the Looshai Campaign in 1871–72, the 4th in East Africa in World War I and the 5th served in the Second Anglo-Sikh War itself. Today, artillery is the second largest arm of the Indian Army, and with its guns, mortars, rocket launchers, unmanned aerial vehicles, surveillance systems, missiles and artillery firepower, it constitutes almost one-sixth of its total strength.

**Q40. The English, who regularly used cannons in their ships, initially used guns landed from their fleet and manned by naval ratings detached for the purpose. They first placed twelve guns near the village of Armegaon along the Coromandel coast. The gunners were called topasses from the word 'tope' in which language?**

A40. Portuguese. In 1668, two companies of the East India Company's artillery were formed in Bombay. The other presidencies followed suit. The power of artillery in defining military power at that time was so pervasive that, initially, the British did not permit the natives to join the artillery arm. As the artillery was expanded and sufficient European recruits could not be mustered, the company gradually permitted the natives to join the artillery in a small percentage. These Indian gunners, recruited as support staff, were called golandaz, gun lashkars, tindals and serangs.

**Did You Know?**

The diagnostic chain Dr Lal Path Labs is run by an alumnus of AFMC, Pune. Dr Arvind Lal is also a Hon. Brig. and Padma Shri awardee.

**Q41. In 1813, Sir Henry Russell, then the British Resident in the court of the Nizam of Hyderabad, raised the Russell Brigade, comprising two battalions. Later, four more battalions were raised and they were known as the Berar Infantry. In addition, two battalions, known as the Elichpur Brigade, were raised by Nawab Salabat Khan, Subedar of Berar, as a part of the Nizam's forces. The men of the Russell Brigade were chiefly Hindus, recruited from Oudh and other parts of Uttar Pradesh. Which modern-day regiment thus traces its origins to this arrangement?**

Kumaon Regiment insignia

A41. The Kumaon Regiment. It is one of the oldest infantry regiments of the Indian Army. The regiment has fought in every major campaign of the British Indian Army and the Indian Army, including the two world wars, and is one of the highest decorated regiments of the Indian Army. The Indian Army's initiative to hold the Siachen Glacier consisted of units of the Kumaon Regiment and the Ladakh Scouts.

**Q42. Raised in 1846, the 15th Ludhiana Sikhs would be entrusted to hold a key holy city during the course of the 1857 mutiny. Despite calls of rebellion from the Bengal Native Infantry and parts of the Sikhs themselves, this key city eluded the control of the rebels in large part due to the instrumental action of the Sikhs. Identify the city.**

Ludhiana Sikhs badge

A42. Varanasi (then Benares). In Benares, the 15th Ludhiana Sikhs was led by a ruthless British officer, Lt Col James Neill, who would later, as a brigadier general, ruthlessly massacre suspected rebels in Kanpur before finally being killed in the storming of Lucknow in 1858.

**Q43. The Ludhiana Sikhs played a key role in the victory of Gen. Roberts over the Afghan forces of Ayub Khan in 1880, finally exacting British vengeance for a humiliating retreat forty-eight years ago. Identify the battle, named after an ancient city named after Alexander the Great and the birthplace of the Taliban.**

Rare coins minted with the British crown and Arabic script in British-occupied Kandahar

A43. Kandahar. The name comes from Iskander, that is, Alexander. The Battle of Kandahar was the final major battle in the Second Anglo-Afghan war that avenged the British massacre of 1842. Ayub Khan was exiled while the British appointee, Abdur Rehman, became the emir after the Treaty of Gandamak.

**Q44. In the Kandahar campaign, the Ludhiana Sikhs were part of the 3rd Infantry Brigade, commanded by a maverick explorer and general. Identify this general, in whose memory a New Delhi think tank, USI, has been awarding medals since 1887 to Indian military personnel for exceptional achievements in exploration, adventure sports and military reconnaissance.**

MacGregor medal

A44. General McGregor. The McGregor Medal is awarded in his memory by the United Services Institute of India, with the first awardee being the legendary Lt Gen. Zorawar Bakshi (awarded the MVC for planning the capture of Hajipir in 1965) for his actions in the reconnaissance of Tibet.

**Q45. The only Victoria Cross from the 15th Ludhiana Sikhs in World War I, this maverick lieutenant, with his ten superhero Sikh mates (only two survived the charge), managed to convey a total of ninety-six bombs within 20 yards of enemy trenches over exceptionally dangerous ground in northern France. Identify this famous British military officer, who later earned a baronetcy. What British military debacle is he infamously known for in World War II, which earned him an immediate dismissal from command by Lord Wavell?**

The Battle of the Sittang Bridge

A45. Brig. Sir John (Jackie) Smyth, 1st Baronet and later MP. As the general officer commanding (GOC), 17th Indian Infantry Division, he became known for his infamous command to blow up the bridge across the Sittang River in Burma while two-thirds of his division was on the other side with no means of escape. This disaster led to the fall of Rangoon to the Japanese, with most of his division taken prisoners of war (POWs), although there is still some controversy regarding culpability for the disaster.

**Q46. A veteran of the Bombay Native Infantry, Col Robert Phayre was a decorated military officer battle-hardened in Afghanistan in 1840, in Sindh in 1843 and in Ethiopia in 1863. He was rewarded with a posting as the resident of a twenty-one-gun salute princely state in 1873. Phayre's personal enmity with the ruler of the state, Malharrao Gaekwad, would ultimately result in an infamous political crisis. Identify this princely state.**

A46. Baroda. It was formed in 1721 when the Maratha general Pilaji Gaekwad conquered Songadh from the Mughals. The state finally joined India in 1949. It gets its name from the Sanskrit word *vatodara*, meaning 'in the heart of the banyan'.

**Q47. Born to a 'bonded labourer' household of Momai Tamuli, he rose to one of the most powerful positions in the Ahom empire. This general would first make his mark while capturing Guwahati from the Mughals in 1667 before a devastating setback in Alboi in 1669. Identify this Assamese icon, in whose memory 24 November is celebrated by the Assamese government.**

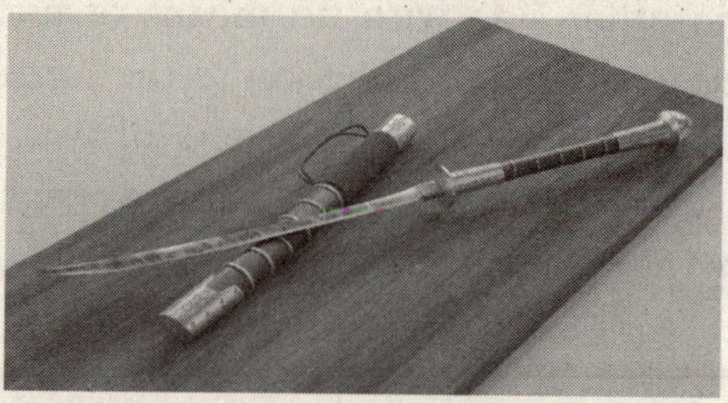

Hengdang sword presented to Lachit after the capture of Guwahati in 1667

A47. Lachit Borphukan.

**Q48. The 1748 Treaty of Aix-la-Chapelle marked the end of the War of the Austrian Succession. One of**

**the terms of the treaty was an exchange of the British-controlled town of Louisbourg in eastern Canada to France in return for what French-controlled settlement in India to be handed back to the British East India Company?**

A48. Chennai. Then known as Madras, the city was captured by French forces in 1746. One of the British defenders who managed to escape the siege and convey the news of the fall of the city to his superiors in Cuddalore was Robert Clive, the infamous East India Company official remembered for defeating Siraj-ud-Daulah at the Battle of Plassey.

**Q49. Which battle, fought in 1760 primarily between the British East India Company and the French East India Company in modern-day Tamil Nadu, resulted in the British capture of settlements like Chetpattu, Thiruvannaamalai and Tindivanam and restricted the French presence in India to Pondicherry?**

A49. The Battle of Wandiwash. The French forces, commanded by Thomas Arthur, Comte de Lally, tried to conquer the fort of Wandiwash from British hands. Their loss in this battle was one of the reasons that compelled the French to sign the Treaty of Paris, effectively diminishing their status in India to little more than traders.

**Q50. The Battle of Delhi was fought in 1803 near the village of Patparganj in East Delhi as part of the Second Anglo-Maratha War. A memorial commemorating this battle was installed nearby and lay forgotten for almost two centuries—when it was discovered hidden between bushes and overgrowth in 1989 during the development of a sporting facility nearby, and spruced up to make the inscription readable. What sporting facility is this, home to a memorial to the Battle of Delhi?**

War Memorial, Noida

A50. Noida Golf Course.

**Did You Know?**

Condoms were used on a large scale to seal mine fuses by specially trained Mukti Bahini divers in the 1971 war.

**Q51. Realizing Mughal numerical superiority on land and relative naval weakness in 1671 under Ram Singh,**

**Lachit Borphukan devised a novel tactic in forcing the Mughals to take the naval route in approaching Guwahati. He lured the Mughal forces to a small hamlet on the northern bank of the Brahmaputra near Guwahati; the ensuing Mughal defeat would be the end of Mughal aspirations in Assam. Which battle was this, named after the town where the first rail-cum-road bridge was constructed over the Brahmaputra in Assam? What is the geographical uniqueness of this location with respect to the Brahmaputra's course, which played a key role in bottling Mughal forces in the kill zone?**

The Battle of Saraighat map

A51. The Battle of Saraighat. It is the place where the Brahmaputra is narrowest in its course. This eliminated any chance of manoeuvrability for Mughal ships as Ahom ships blockaded them from both sides. After the targeted elimination of Munawwar, the Mughal admiral in charge, Ahoms used special bridges to board the Mughal boats and the tide of the war was turned. Lachit is said to have been seriously ill before the beginning of the battle but still led from the front in the finale. He died shortly after the war from the illness in 1672.

# Section 2

## India at the World Wars and in the Years Between

The Indian Army saw a spate of reforms and reorganization from 1878 till the start of the First World War. A massive effort was put into the Alliance effort by this well-trained army—one that was better aligned to the functioning of the western armies than ever before. The army saw action in virtually all theatres—Europe, the Mediterranean, the Middle East and Africa—and was the largest voluntary army of the conflict, with nearly 1.3 million participants. Of these, 62,000 died and another 67,000 were wounded. The war saw Indian soldiers being awarded the Victoria Cross for the first time ever, suffering untold misery in the trenches of Flanders Field, starving to death in Mesopotamia due to poor leadership and guarding vital oil fields all across the Middle East. But they performed very admirably throughout the war, ensuring that the British were forced to open up officer positions for Indians after the war ended.

The intervening years saw Indians graduating in ever-larger numbers from the military and Royal Air Force (RAF) academies, taking on staff appointments and doing exceptionally well at all the tasks given to them. The result was that by the time the Second World War started, a number of these men had acquired the respect of their western counterparts and were a vital part of the planning and organization of the Allied war machinery.

By September 1939, India, as a part of the Allied Nations, sent over two and a half million soldiers to fight under British command against the Axis powers. India also provided the base for American operations in support of China in the China Burma India Theatre. A large number of air bases created in those days continue to form the backbone of the Eastern Air Command of the Indian Air Force (IAF) till date. Once again, Indians fought with great distinction all across the globe. They distinguished themselves in the deserts of North Africa as much as in the Burmese jungles and the icy mountains of Italy. Once again, over 87,000 Indian troops and three million civilians died in World War II. A unique feature of this war was the participation of the Indian National Army (INA) led by Subhash Chandra Bose, who used Indian volunteers and POWs to form his own army to take on the British colonialists. The contribution of this force too needs to be remembered by future generations. The words of Field Marshal Sir Claude Auchinleck, former commander-in-chief, India, probably express it best—he said that Britain 'couldn't have come through both wars (World War I and II) if they hadn't had the Indian Army.' This section delves into some known and some unknown facets of the Indian Army during this tumultuous period.

**Q1. After having raided the town of Shaikh Said in Yemen and then defending the Suez Canal in early 1915, which military campaign did the 29th Indian Brigade take part in?**

Indian soldiers at Gallipoli

A1. The Gallipoli Campaign. This was a military campaign during the First World War which unfolded on the Gallipoli peninsula in modern Turkey in 1915. Britain, France and Russia sought to weaken the Ottoman Empire by taking control of the Turkish Straits. The 29th Indian Brigade, including the 1/6th Gurkha Rifles, landed, took and secured Sari Bair above the landing beaches and was joined by the 1/5th Gurkha Rifles and the 2/10th Gurkha Rifles.

**Q2. Keeping the Germans from advancing beyond the Hollebeke sector with his relentless machine-gun firing during the First Battle of Ypres in Belgium, which Indian soldier was the first Indian to win the Victoria Cross?**

A2. Subedar Khudadad Khan. Fighting for the British Indian Army, he was a recipient of the Victoria Cross, the highest wartime gallantry award given to British and Commonwealth forces.

**Q3. Who wrote *Across the Black Waters*, a 1939 English novel describing the experiences of Lalu, an Indian sepoy fighting on behalf of the Allied Forces against the Germans in France during World War I?**

A3. Mulk Raj Anand. The book is part of a trilogy (along with *The Village* and *The Sword and the Sickle*) chronicling the life of Lalu as he struggles to rise from the bottom of Indian society. In the background is India's fight for independence. This book is the only major Indian-English novel set amidst the First World War.

**Q4. This thirty-year-old lady of Indian and American descent was born in Moscow in 1914. A descendant of Tipu Sultan, she became a British heroine of World War II, renowned for her service in the Women's Auxiliary Air Force and the Special Operations Executive. She fought behind enemy lines in France, where she was betrayed and arrested by the Nazis. Who was she?**

A4. Noor Inayat Khan. She was awarded the George Cross for her services. She died at the infamous Dachau concentration camp in Germany, where a small memorial to her still stands.

**Q5: Nilkanth Shriram Jatar, born in Pune in 1887, fondly called Bhausaheb, served in the First World War. A highly decorated officer, which corps did he serve in during The Great War?**

A5. The Medical Corps or the Indian Medical Service. Educated at Seth G.S. Medical College, he completed his MRCS in London and became the Medical Officer to the 16th Cavalry in the Turkish axis. He commanded the unit in battle when his commander fell. He was a prisoner of war between 1916 and 1918 at Kut El Amara, braving inhuman conditions and a typhus outbreak. He earned a DSO and was also decorated with the Serbian Order of the White Eagle with Swords. In 1920, he was deployed in Waziristan, where he sustained bullet wounds to his right leg and underwent an amputation. He was awarded a bar to his DSO and decorated with the Order of the Companion of the Indian Empire. Fitted with a prosthetic at the age of thirty-two, he served as the Inspector General of Prisons, Central Provinces and Berar. His sons too went on to become, respectively, an AVM, a major general and a brigadier.

**Q6. Mir Dast and Mir Mast were two Pashtun brothers from Tirah Valley who fought in the First World War. What was their unique claim to fame?**

A6. The two brothers served on different sides during the First World War! While Mir Dast was decorated with the Victoria Cross for leading his platoon when no British officers were left during the Second Battle of Ypres, his brother was disgraced by the British for having defected to the German side.

**Q7. Which structure, originally built as a seaside retreat for George, Prince of Wales (later King George IV) and expanded by John Nash in 1815 in the Indo-Saracenic style, was transformed into a hospital for Indian soldiers during World War I?**

Royal Pavilion, Brighton

A7. The Royal Pavilion, Brighton. From December 1914 to January 1916, sick and wounded soldiers from the Indian Army were treated in this former palace. The structure, among other reasons, was chosen for the supposed comfort that its domes and minarets would provide to the recouping soldiers.

**Q8. This company was run by the Tenth USAAF for a few years and was designated 84th Air Depot. For some years, it also built railway carriages. Founded in 1940, it was bought out by the Government of India in 1942 because it was deemed to be a strategic asset that was to be destroyed lest it fall into Japanese hands. What corporation/company was this?**

A8. Hindustan Aeronautics Limited. After initially being founded by Hirachand Walchand with an American, Mr Pawley, and funding/support from the State of Mysore, the company was bought out by the British government. The first aircraft to be overhauled was a Consolidated PBY Catalina, followed by every type of aircraft operated in India and Burma.

**Q9. In 1917, he became the first Indian to join the Royal Flying Corps (RFC) during World War I. He flew the Sopwith Camel fighter jets and shot down eight German fighters before taking a hit, but still continued fighting. His aircraft counted over 400 bullet holes. Who was this 'Flying Sikh', the first Indian pilot ever?**

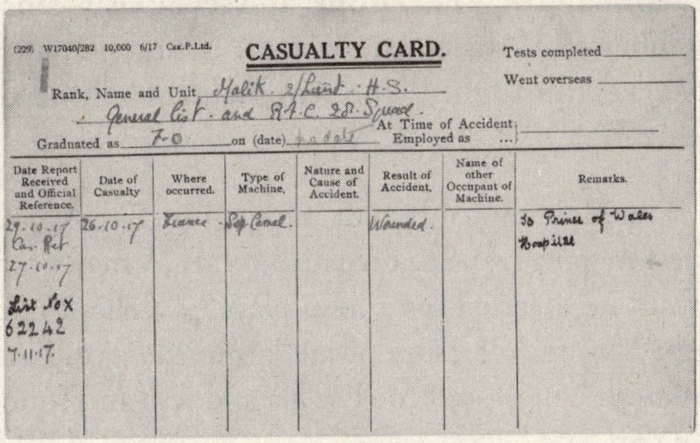

(229) W17040/282 10,000 6/17 Cax.P.Ltd.

**CASUALTY CARD.**

Tests completed

Went overseas

Rank, Name and Unit Malik. 2/Lieut. H.S.
General List. and R.F.C. 28. Squad.

Graduated as F.O. on (date)

At Time of Accident Employed as ...

| Date Report Received and Official Reference. | Date of Casualty | Where occurred. | Type of Machine. | Nature and Cause of Accident. | Result of Accident. | Name of other Occupant of Machine. | Remarks. |
|---|---|---|---|---|---|---|---|
| 29.10.17 Cas. Ret 27.10.17 List No X 62242 7.11.17. | 26.10.17 | France | Sop Camel. | | Wounded. | | to Prince of Wales Hospital |

Hardit Singh Malik's Casualty Card

A9. Sardar (Lt) Hardit Singh Malik. A graduate of Balliol College, Oxford, he had blues in cricket and golf. He staunchly refused to part with his turban and somehow managed to fit over it an outsized flying helmet, earning the affectionate nickname of 'Flying Hobgoblin' from the ground crews. Later, he was prime minister of Patiala State and then ambassador to Canada and France.

**Q10. Two Bleriot monoplanes came to India via ship in November 1910, were transported via train to Allahabad and then assembled and flown in the polo ground for the first time in India by Keith Davies on 10 December 1910. Along with them came two Farman biplanes. It had been just two years since the**

**first aeroplane flew in Europe, and seven years since 17 December 1903, when the Wright Brothers made the first successful flight. Who was the man behind these endeavours?**

A10. The Maharaja of Patiala, Bhupendra Singh. He was the first man in India to own an aircraft. A man of many interests, he married ten times, played excellent cricket, had the largest collection of medals in the world at one point, built a monorail for Patiala and was an Honorary Lt Gen. in 1931.

Patiala airfield was an instrumental set-up for the completion of flying training of all pilot officers in training. The days before the Air Force Academy was instituted, Jodhpur and Patiala formed the basis of flying training, both airfields set up by their aviation enthusiast maharajas.

**Did You Know?**

Lt Col Joyscilla Farida Rehana, a doctor, was the first woman to become a paratrooper in the Indian Army in 1966.

**Q11. He was the first Indian to be awarded the Distinguished Flying Cross (DFC) for his successful operations against the Germans. He shot down far better aircraft before his own was shot down, causing his tragic death. He used to fly the 'Scouting Experimental' (SE5 and SE5A). Who was this?**

A11. Lt Indra Lal Roy. The only Indian Flying Ace during World War I, he is credited with ten victories. Roy was killed over Carvin on 22 July 1918 in a dog fight against the Fokker D.VIIs of Jagdstaffel 29, before he had even turned twenty.

**Q12. The No. 1 Squadron, which was initially equipped with Westland Wapitis, saw the induction of Lysanders in September 1941. Why was the squadron also known as the Bombay Squadron thereafter?**

A12. On 7 November 1941, twelve Lysanders were presented to No. 1 Squadron by the Governor of Bombay as the citizens of Bombay sponsored their purchase and No. 1 Squadron was considered adopted by Bombay from that day onwards. Sir Homi Mehta of Bombay, a staunch supporter of aviation in India, led a group of industrialists and citizens to create the Bombay Governor's War Gifts Fund, which donated Rs 30,00,000 to buy the Lysanders, which were named Bombay City I, II, III, IV, Satara, Konkan, Sholapur and Gujarat. One of the officers designed the crest of No. 1 Squadron with a tiger symbol and the motto '*Ittehad mein shakti hai* (In unity lies strength)'.

**Q13. The first set of Indian cadets at Cranwell Air Force Academy reached there on 4 September 1930. These included H.C. Sircar, Jagat Narain Tandon, Bhupinder Singh, Subroto Mukherjee, Amarjit**

**Singh and Aiyad Baksh Awan. All of them were from influential families of India. How were the two Singhs connected to the history of New Delhi?**

A13. They were from a rich Punjabi family. Their uncle was Sardar Bahadur Sir Shobha Singh, pioneer builder of New Delhi. They were from Government College, Lahore. Aiyad Baksh Awan also came from the same college. Harish Chandra Sircar was from St Stephen's College, Delhi. Subroto Mukherjee passed out from Presidency College, Calcutta, and was studying in England. He was the nephew of the late Lt Indra Lal Roy, DFC. Jagat Narain Tandon, from Christian College, Lucknow, was a small-built man who was transferred to the Equipment and Stores Branch in December 1930 because he was too short to reach the rudder bar and to see out of the cockpit. He thus became the first ground duty officer of the IAF.

**Q14. The initial years of the IAF were full of tragedy and setbacks. Bhupinder Singh and Amarjit Singh died in an air accident in September 1933. H.C. Sircar left the IAF after a couple of years. He was dismissed from service following an unfortunate accident that claimed the lives of soldiers on the ground. Jagat Tandon died during World War Two. A.B. Awan left the IAF in 1945. Aspy Merwan Engineer, even though he was the winner of the prestigious R.M. Groves flying prize, also had the distinction of being the first**

**Indian to earn the Caterpillar Club membership. Which 'unfortunate' action of his allowed him entry to this club?**

A14. He was the first Indian to bail out of an aircraft using a parachute. The Caterpillar Club is an informal association of people who have successfully used a parachute to bail out of a disabled aircraft. The name 'Caterpillar Club' refers to the silk threads that made the original parachutes, thus recognizing the debt owed to the silkworm. Other people have taken the metaphor further by comparing the act of bailing out with that of the caterpillar letting itself down to earth by a silken thread. Another metaphor is that caterpillars have to climb out of their cocoons to escape. 'Life depends on a silken thread' is the club's motto.

**Q15. The IAF Voluntary Reserve (IAFVR) was created during World War II to provide the manpower to defend the coastal borders of the country as the RAF units were deployed in the war. The Coastal Defence Flights (CDF) were formed at the major ports of the country: Juhu (Bombay), St Thomas Mount (Madras), Dum Dum (Calcutta), Drigh Road and Willingdon Island. Which cities were served by the last two?**

A15. Karachi and Kochi. The first set of IAFVR pilot officers was commissioned in November 1939 and went on to play significant roles in future. These included

Surjit Singh Majithia (later deputy defence minister, India), Rup Chand, Hem Chaudhary, Dhrubendra Bhanj Deo (heir to the State of Mayurbhanj, Bengal; killed in action over the Bay of Bengal against Japan), Kundan Lal Sondhi, Kalyan Rajan Das, Pratap Chandra Lal (later Chief of Air Staff), Bhupinder Singh Dugal, Abdul Morad, Hiranand Mansukhani, Murzban Choksey, Jehangir Engineer, Ramaswami Tyabji, Habib Tyabji and Noshir Gazdar.

**Q16. Tulbahadur Pun was a rifleman in the 6 Gurkha Rifles of the Indian Army during the Second World War. His heroic actions on 23 June 1944 saw him being awarded the Victoria Cross. How was he posthumously memorialized in 2021 at Paddington Station in London?**

Train named in honour of Gurkha legend Tulbahadur VC

A16. An inter-city train was named after him by Great Western Railway. It is an honour usually reserved for kings, queens and castles. The ceremony was attended by the actress Dame Joanna Lumley, whose father, Maj. James Lumley, was the commanding officer of Tulbahadur Pun in 6 Gurkha Rifles.

**Q17. Madhukar Srinagesh, Ajit Nath and Parmeshwar Khurana were commissioned as flying officers in July–August 1940. Into what branch of the IAF were these the first inductees?**

A17. The Medical Branch. They were the first doctors of the Indian Air Force. Trained in aviation medicine in the USA, AVM M.M. Srinagesh OBE was a keen practitioner of the then-fledgling speciality of aerospace medicine. He retired from the IAF at the rank of air vice-marshal on 10 September 1971. Ajit Nath was the first medical officer of the No. 1 Squadron of the IAF. Trained in aviation medicine in the UK, France, Italy and Germany, he contributed greatly to the formation of the Aero Medical Society and School of Aviation Medicine.

**Q18. On 22 March 1943, *Life* magazine carried an article that featured some photos of an Indo-American venture whose roots lay in China. The article said, 'In the industrial desert of India, American enterprise has produced one first-class ________ factory. It is William Pawley's _______ _______ _____ and naturally it is in India's most progressive state, Mysore, which has plenty of electric power, steel and semi-skilled labor.' Which enterprise was being written about here?**

A18. Hindustan Aircraft Limited in Bangalore. Its founder and president, William Douglas Pawley, for seven years owned China's only plane factory and sold China $30,000,000 worth of planes and services. When the Japanese last bombed his plant near the border of Burma, he had already moved the machinery and equipment out to Mysore. This factory assembled Vultee and Curtiss-type ships and produced Harlow trainers. In less than two years, it had equipped itself to repair all American planes and had dug out a channel for flying boats. HAL was Pawley's joint venture with the Walchands, Mysore State and the Government of India.

**Q19. Fondly called 'Jumbo', he was the first Indian to reach the rank of Wing Commander. He won the Distinguished Flying Cross twice. Because of his superb piloting skills and indomitable spirit, Life magazine featured him in its issue dated 15 May 1944 among twelve of the world's most outstanding airmen. What connected this Jumbo to Op Polo in Hyderabad?**

A19. Jumbo was Wg Cdr Karun Krishna Majumdar. His cousin was Jayanto Nath Chaudhuri, the man who led the forces in Op Polo. Chaudhuri later became the sixth Chief of Army Staff. Jumbo tragically died in an air crash during a show near Lahore aged just thirty-one.

**Q20. On 7 September 1930, five cadets from India entered the RAF academy at Cranwell for training. They finished training on 20 July 1932 and after a short leave, reported to No. 16 Army Cooperation Squadron RAF at Old Sarum on 16 August 1932, holding the rank of pilot officer in the IAF. What was strange about this event?**

A20. The IAF was officially formed only on 8 October 1932, while its first set of pilots was commissioned on 15 August 1932! These pilot officers, popularly known as 'Pip Os', moved to India to form the nucleus of the No. 1 Squadron, which was born on 1 April 1933.

**Q21. 1 April 1933 was the day that the No. 1 Squadron of the IAF was formed and was celebrated as IAF Day. Then, twenty-one years later, Air Marshal Subroto Mukherjee took over as the first Indian chief of the air staff on the same date. The anniversary was celebrated every year with one exception. The forty-third anniversary was never celebrated. Why?**

A21. Air Force Day was shifted from 1 April to 8 October. It was on 8 October 1932 that the governor general approved the IAF Act, which brought the service into existence. This changeover was promulgated on 11 March 1976 and so the forty-third-anniversary celebrations never took place. Instead, on 8 October 1976, the forty-fourth anniversary was celebrated keeping in mind the date of the IAF Act. Incidentally, Subroto Mukherjee had been commissioned on 8 October 1932!

**Q22. Each year, 1 May is commemorated as Armour Day in the Indian Army. It was on this date in 1938 that a certain regiment dismounted from their horses and moved to tanks. The first equipment inducted were the Vickers Light Tanks and the Chevrolet Armoured Cars. Which regiment was this?**

A22. Scinde Horse. Raised in Sindh, now part of Pakistan, it was part of the Bombay Army. It was raised in 1839 to protect the Spice Route from the Bolan Pass to Sukkur on the Indus River to Bikaner, Hissar and then Delhi. Protection was needed against the marauding Baluchi warriors, especially the Jekhrani tribesmen.

**Q23. The Chindits, officially called Long Range Penetration Groups, were special operations units of the British and Indian armies which saw action in 1943–44 during the Burma Campaign of World War II. The British Army Brigadier Orde Wingate formed the Chindits for raiding operations against the Imperial Japanese Army, especially long-range penetration, attacking Japanese troops, facilities and lines of communication deep behind Japanese lines. Their operations featured long marches through extremely difficult terrain, undertaken by underfed**

**troops often weakened by diseases such as malaria and dysentery. How did the group get its name, the Chindits?**

Chindits patch

A23. The name Chindits is a corrupted form of *chinthe*, the Burmese word for 'lion'. This was the badge adopted by the group. During the East African Campaign of 1940–41, Wingate—under General Archibald Wavell, commander-in-chief of the Middle East Command—had begun to explore guerrilla tactics when he created and commanded a unit known as Gideon Force, composed of regular troops from Sudan and Ethiopia, as well as Ethiopian partisans. Gideon Force disrupted Italian supply lines and collected intelligence.

In 1942, after the disbandment of Gideon Force, Wavell—who had since been appointed commander-in-chief of the India Command—requested the services of Wingate in Burma. It was intended that he would raise irregular forces to operate behind the Japanese lines, in a manner similar to Gideon Force. Controversy persists over the extremely high casualty rate and the debatable military value of the achievements of the Chindits.

**Q24. The Japanese plan to invade India, code-named U-Go, was originally intended as a spoiling attack against the British IV Corps at Imphal in Manipur, to disrupt the Allied offensive plans for that year. The commander of the Japanese Fifteenth Army, Lt Gen. Renya Mutaguchi, enlarged the plan to invade India itself and perhaps even overthrow the British Raj. However, his plans failed as a result of resolute action by Indian troops in a battle that has been referred to by authors such as Martin Dougherty and Jonathan Ritter as the 'Stalingrad of the East'. Which battle was this?**

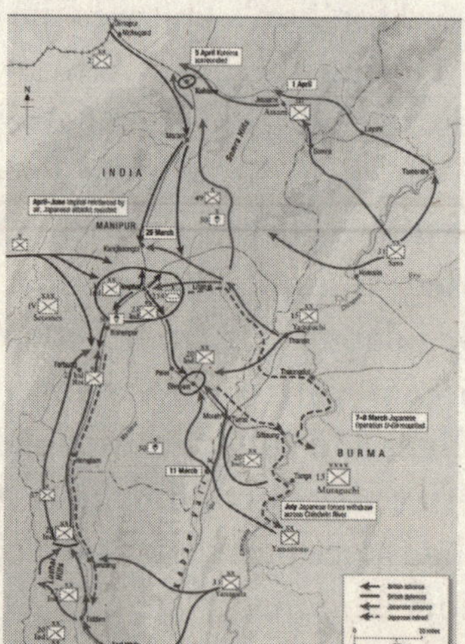


The Battle of Kohima map

A24. The Battle of Kohima. The battle took place in three stages from 4 April to 22 June 1944 around the town of Kohima, now the capital city of Nagaland in north-east India. From 4 to 16 April, the Japanese attempted to capture Kohima ridge. By mid-April, the small British and Indian force at Kohima was relieved. From 18 April to 13 May, British and Indian reinforcements counter-attacked to drive the Japanese from the positions they had captured. The Japanese abandoned the ridge at this point but continued to block the Kohima-Imphal road. From 16 May to 22 June, the British and Indian troops pursued the retreating Japanese and reopened the road. The battle ended on 22 June when British and Indian troops from Kohima and Imphal met at Milestone 109, ending the Siege of Imphal.

Military historian Robert Lyman said that the battle of Kohima and Imphal 'changed the course of the Second World War in Asia . . . For the first time, the Japanese were defeated in a battle and they never recovered from it.' In 2013, a poll conducted by the British National Army Museum voted the Battles of Kohima and Imphal as 'Britain's Greatest Battle'.

**Q25. Part of the Battle of Imphal, this battle took place in Manipur between 20 and 26 March 1944. The Japanese under Maj. Gen. Miyazaki fought the 50th Indian Parachute Brigade in a bloody encounter that**

**resulted in over 650 dead among the Indian brigade and over 400 Japanese casualties. More significantly, it delayed the Japanese advance by a week. Which famous battle was this?**

A25. The Battle of Sangshak. The 50th Parachute Brigade had been raised in October 1941 and later was one of two parachute brigades in the 44th Indian Airborne Division. The actions at Sangshak resulted in the Allies getting time to reinforce the defences of Imphal. This eventually proved crucial in the outcome of the overall battle for Kohima and Imphal. The unit saw action in Kashmir in 1948, in Goa in 1961 and also in 1971.

**Q26. Often called the Battle of Sinzweya or the Battle of Ngakyedauk, this battle took place in the Burma Campaign from 5 to 23 February 1944. Over 5000 Japanese perished in the battle, while Allied losses were also in excess of 3500. The battle gets its more popular name from the makeshift rectangular defensive position of Maj. Gen. Frank Messervy and his staff. What was its name?**

A26. The Battle of the Admin Box. Brig. Geoffrey Evans, who was commander of the 9th Indian Infantry Brigade, part of the 5th Indian Division, assumed command and held the box against all attacks. The defenders were joined by part of the 4th Battalion of the 8th Gurkha Rifles. Under Evans, the box was converted into a defended area. The clearing measured a bare 1200 yards (1.1 km) in diameter. Ammunition dumps were piled up at the foot of the western face of a central hillock, 150 feet (46 m) high, named 'Ammunition Hill'. On the ground, the fighting for the Admin Box was severe and, for the most part, hand-to-hand. Although the total Allied casualties were higher than the Japanese, the Japanese had been forced to abandon many of their wounded to die. For the first time in the Burma campaign, the Japanese tactics had been countered and, indeed, turned against them. This was to be repeated on a far larger scale in the impending Battle of Imphal.

**Q27. The 950th (Indian) Infantry Regiment was a military unit raised during the Second World War, initially as part of the German Army and later the Waffen-SS from August 1944 onwards. Intended to serve as a liberation force for British-ruled India, it was made up of Indian prisoners of war and expatriates in Europe. Due to its origins in the Indian independence movement, it was also known as the 'Tiger Legion' and 'Azad Hind Fauj'. As part of the Waffen-SS, it was known as the Indian Volunteer Legion. However, where was the Azad Hindustan Battalion created in February 1942?**

A27. Italy. This unit constituted Indian POWs from their Centro I POW camp and Italians previously resident in India and Persia and ultimately served under the Raggruppamento Centri Militari alongside units of Arabs and colonial Italians. However, the effort had little acceptance from the Indians in the unit, who did not wish to serve under Italian officers. After the Italian loss at the Second Battle of El Alamein, the Indians mutinied when told to fight in Libya. Consequently, the remnants of the battalion were disbanded in November 1942.

**Q28. On the night of 17 February 1944, the main assault of this battle took place. The 4/6th Rajputana Rifles would go along Snakeshead Ridge with the 1/9th Gurkha Rifles and the 1/2nd Gurkha Rifles in a direct assault on the monastery. The fighting was brutal, but no progress was made and casualties were heavy. The Rajputanas lost 196 officers and men, the 1/9th Gurkhas 149 and the 1/2nd Gurkhas ninety-six. It became clear that the attack had failed and on 18 February, Dimoline and Freyberg called off the attacks on Monastery Hill. There were a number of similar attempts over the next few weeks. In their time on the front line, the 4th Indian Division had lost 3000 men and the 2nd New Zealand Division suffered 1600 men killed,**

**missing and wounded. Which iconic battle of the Second World War was this?**

A28. The Battle of Monte Cassino, also known as the Battle for Rome. It consisted of a series of four assaults made by the Allies against German forces in Italy during the Italian Campaign. The aim was to break through the Winter Line and facilitate an advance towards Rome. Between 17 January and 18 May, Monte Cassino and the Gustav defences were attacked on four separate occasions by Allied troops. Following the Allied victory, the German Senger Line collapsed on 25 May, and the German defenders were driven from their positions. The capture of Monte Cassino resulted in 55,000 Allied casualties, with German losses estimated at around 20,000 killed and wounded. In the course of the battles, the ancient abbey of Monte Cassino, where St Benedict, in 516 AD, first established the rule that ordered monasticism in the West, was entirely destroyed by Allied bombing and artillery barrages in February 1944.

**Q29. First coming to attention in Jessore in 1824, this disease had mystified doctors across the North-east and Bengal. In 1901, while examining the spleen of a dead soldier in Dum Dum, Calcutta, a pioneering future director general of the Army Medical Corps would discover oval bodies in the spleen that would**

**finally solve the mystery of the so-called 'Assam Fever'. Identify the disease and the doctor.**

Lt Gen. W.B. Leishman

A29. Kala-azar or Leishmaniasis, and Lt Gen. (Dr) William Boog Leishman, after whom the disease is named. It is also called Dum Dum fever since Leishman discovered it in the Dum Dum patient. Another army medical officer and explorer, Charles Donovan, independently discovered similar oval bodies in 1903, thus leading to them being called LD (Leishman Donovan) bodies, which are diagnostic of kala-azar.

**Q30. The causative parasite genus of kala-azar was named after Lt Gen. Leishman by an illustrious Nobel laureate who was impressed by his work, thus immortalizing him in modern parasitology. Who was this Nobel laureate?**

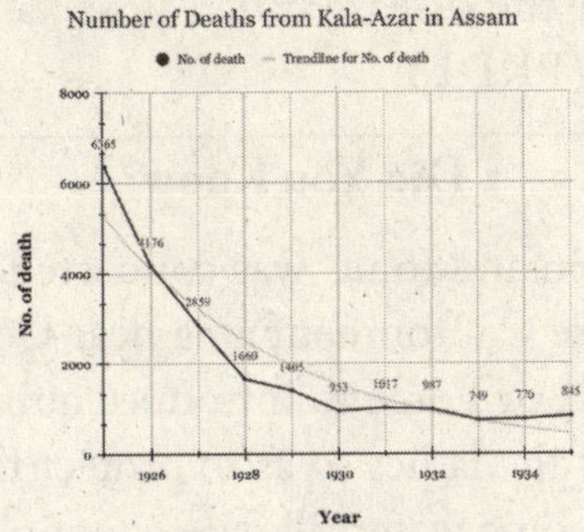


Number of deaths from kala-azar in Assam

Dr Upendranath Brahmachari

A30. Ronald Ross, the 1902 Nobel Prize winner for the discovery of the causative agent of malaria. Dr Upendranath Brahmachari, a two-time Nobel Prize nominee in physiology, in 1929 and 1942, discovered urea stibamine, which drastically reduced the death rate in Assam caused by kala-azar. He also discovered a rare form of the disease called post kala-azar dermal leishmaniasis (PKDL).

> **Did You Know?**
>
> The 'gin and tonic' was concocted in the Bangalore Cantonment area near Command Hospital Air Force to introduce quinine into the diet of the ladies so as to protect them from malaria. Tonic water till date contains quinine!

**Q31. Lt Gen. Leishman is known chiefly for his work on kala-azar, but his most important contribution is to wartime public health in World War I. Along with Sir Almoth Wright, despite facing strong opposition from conservatives, what did Lt Gen. Leishman help in popularizing in the British Army after successful mass clinical trials in India?**

A31. The anti-typhoid vaccine. Typhoid killed more British soldiers in the Boer War than the enemy. Yet, due to anti-vaxxer pressure during World War I, anti-typhoid vaccination remained voluntary. Smallpox remained the only disease that had mandatory vaccination in the British Army. In the French Army, vaccination against typhoid was mandated. As the war progressed, a new type of infection, called paratyphoid, started causing morbidity, leading to the development of a new vaccine in 1916. This was called the TAB vaccine (against typhoid and paratyphoid A, B) and has remained in use for over a century.

**Q32. The date of 14 April 1944 became a historic day for the town of Moirang in Manipur, the HQ of a 26,000-strong force comprising former POWs of the British Indian Army by a symbolic act of Col Shaukat Malik. Which was this iconic force that played a key role in convincing Gen. Mutaguchi to launch the Indian campaign? Which historic act was this?**

INA Memorial in Moirang with INA motto of '*Ittefaq, ittemad, qurbani*'

A32. Subhash Chandra Bose's Azad Hind Fauj, and the first time the national flag was hoisted on the Indian mainland after Netaji hoisted the tricolour in 1943 in the Gymkhana Club, Port Blair.

**Q33. A key member of the INA who attended the Moirang flag hoisting was a local lad, Mairembam, who would achieve a notable first in Manipuri history. Colloquially named after his home town, what notable first would Mairembam achieve?**

A33. He became the first elected CM of Manipur in 1967—Mairembam Koireng Singh, popularly called

'Moirang Koireng'. Moirang is a very important town for the Meitei people as the origin of their seven cycles of incarnation in Meitei mythology as well as the location of the famous Laila Majnu-ish love story of Khamba Thoibi.

**Q34. The fiercest battle in the entire Burma campaign was fought from 8 April to 12 May 1944 near the grounds of the Kohima District Commissioner's bungalow. Named after a sports facility in the DC bungalow campus, identify this battle, in which a small Commonwealth force held out against waves of a Japanese division attack.**

The Battle of Tennis Court

Tennis Court then and now

A34. The 'Battle of Tennis Court', was named after the tennis court complex located within the bungalow, which saw the heaviest fighting. The tennis court has a cherry tree that saw the maximum casualties, hence the Battle of Tennis Court was also called the 'Battle under Cherry Tree'.

**Q35. In the initial days of the Battle of Kohima, a rifleman of the 1st battalion of an Indian regiment died. The pragmatic unit quartermaster did not report it to HQ and the unit kept getting rations for the dead rifleman. When it was under siege in Kohima, this airdropped extra ration was a decisive factor in the unit's low attrition rate. Two years later, Maj. M.T. Proktor composed a song set to the tune of the *American Battle Hymn of the Republic* to honour this unsung rifleman, quite literally narrating the story. Which foot-stomping regimental song thus came into being?**

Rhino hat

One-horned rhino (only found in Kaziranga National Park, Assam)

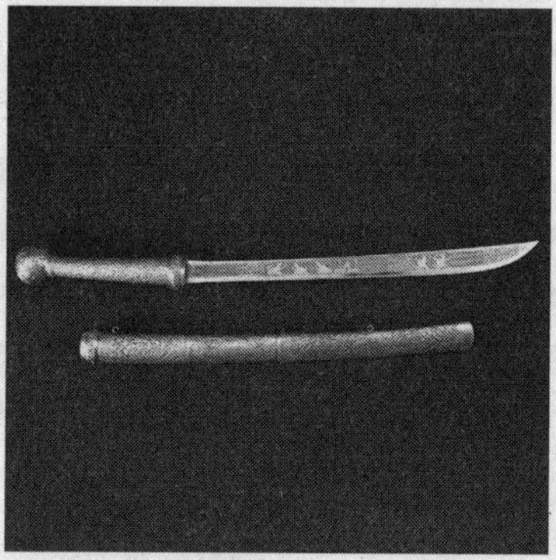

Dah sword

A35. *Badluram Ka Badan* of the Assam Regiment. The Assam Regiment wears the distinctive rhino hat in their uniform and carries the dah sword. Much before Vicky Kaushal made 'How's the *josh*' famous in the film *Uri*, their CO, Maj. Gen. Barbora had come up with the Assam regiment greeting '*Tagra Raho*'. During the commissioning of each new batch in Happy Valley, Shillong (HQ of the Assam Regiment), a rendition of *Badluram Ka Badan* is essential.

**Q36. Simonides of Ceos was a Greek lyrical poet known for commemorating the fallen warriors in the Battle of Thermopylae with these famous lines:**

**'Tell them Lacedaemonians, passerby,**
**That here obedient to their word, we lie.'**
**This would inspire John Maxwell Edmonds, a famous English classicist poet, to come up with a few lines that have been immortalized as a touching ode to fallen soldiers. Which lines are these? Where can one find them etched—a dedication to the fallen soldiers of the Allied 2nd Division?**

Kohima War Memorial

A36. 'When you go home, tell them of us and say, For your tomorrow, we gave our today': Kohima War Memorial, maintained by the Commonwealth Graves Commission (CWGC). 917 Hindu and Sikh soldiers, whose names are mentioned in the memorial, were cremated as per their wishes in the war. Field Marshal William Slim, commander of the 14th Army in Burma, inaugurated this memorial.

**Q37. The lower end of the memorial has the famous Kohima cenotaph (in the picture with the previous question), which is dedicated to the 2nd Division. It is a 15-foot (4.6-metre) tall massive stone. This stone was originally located on a spur at Maram, to the south of Kohima, and was then shifted with the help of the Naga people to be erected at the 2nd British Division's war cemetery. Which intriguing local custom is it based on?**

A37. Naga megalithic headstones—a burial practice of Naga tribes who placed such headstones after the burial of notable members of the tribe.

**Q38. On 21 October 1943, Subhash Chandra Bose announced the formation of the Provisional Government of Free India (*Arz-e-hukumat-e-azad-hind*) from Singapore. Recognized by Japan, Germany, Austria and Ireland, the Japanese government honoured this move by handing over a group of occupied islands to the Azad Hind Fauj that would eventually be named 'Shaheed' and 'Swaraj' by Bose. How do we better know these islands?**

A38. The Andaman and Nicobar Islands. On Parakram Diwas, that is, 23 January 2023, twenty-one of the

Andaman and Nicobar islands were named after the twenty-one PVC awardees.

**Q39. What was the Special Forces division of the Azad Hind Fauj known as?**

A39. Bahadur Group. They were trained in guerrilla warfare, subversion, sabotage behind enemy lines and linguistics. They were often used as pathfinders in the Japanese divisions, and their mastery over languages allowed them to converse with the locals as well as the Japanese. This group followed the first such endeavour by Col Shaukat Malik. Having served in the Bahawalpur State Forces in World War II, he later created the first Intelligence Directorate in the INA. Incidentally, Col Malik was credited with raising the tricolour for the first time on Indian soil, on 14 April 1944, at Moirang with the Leaping Tiger of the INA flash across the standard!

**Did You Know?**

Chetak helicopters were dressed as elephants during the Republic Day Parade flypast in the 1970s to show India's military might and cultural diversity. They also paid homage to Maharana Pratap's steed who wore an elephant armour to spook the opponents' animals.

# Section 3

## Wars of Independent India: A Phoenix Rises from the Ashes

In 1947, at the stroke of the midnight hour, as the nation awoke to a new dawn, it also meant that a significant portion of our defence forces was handed over to West and East Pakistan as agreed. The Indian Armed Forces did not have much time to recuperate as they were sent forthwith into the Kashmir theatre when Pakistani irregulars raided the valley. A valiant effort preserved the Valley but ended in a ceasefire line that allotted areas to Pakistan-occupied Kashmir (PoK).

The nation pushed to reduce the might of the military in line with the philosophy of *ahimsa*, with a police force for internal security, but the armed forces grew from strength to strength despite the bounds placed on them, successfully defending the country against Pakistan in 1948, 1965 and 1999. In 1971, they were instrumental in putting a stop to the genocide of Bengalis and the birth of the fastest-growing South Asian country, Bangladesh.

While the 1962 Sino-Indian War taught us some hard lessons, it emboldened us to take steps to prepare better and train harder to protect the motherland. The Indian Army not only united the country, annexing Hyderabad and liberating Goa but also prevented the Balkanization of the state through multiple internal security conflicts on multiple fronts as our neighbours sought to act via proxies.

Robust politico-military execution managed to prevent India from bleeding through a thousand cuts, but it never caused the dissolution of the separation of the State and the military, leading to a coup, even as Pakistan regularly devolved into coups.

Today, the Indian Armed Forces are poised to strike in conflict, help in disaster and preserve peace, from frigid Siachen to the warm maritime boundary of our peninsula, from the marshes of Kutch to the unforgiving jungles of the North-east.

**Q1. During the Battle of Longewala, the Pakistani armoured thrust on 4–5 December 1971 on India's western borders aimed to capture which city in Rajasthan? What was its objective?**

A1. Jaisalmer. They aimed to neutralize the key air force base located there.

**Q2. Deluded by the relative success of the Kutch conflict, President Ayub Khan of Pakistan, egged on by his foreign minister Zulfikar Ali Bhutto, approved a plan on 13 May 1965 in Murree to resolve the Kashmir issue once and for all without provoking an all-out war. The Pakistani top brass believed that the Kashmiri Muslims would wholeheartedly support their religious brethren from across the border in an insurrection against the Indian state. That would then give Pakistan a reason to intervene officially. What was the name of the operation?**

A2. Operation Gibraltar. They named this operation after a British-controlled strategic European city which was once used by the Umayyads for a holy war to capture Spain.

**Q3. On the last day of the 1965 war, a thirty-six-year-old IAF Hawker Hunter pilot was shot down by ground fire over Kasur. After learning his identity,**

**Ayub Khan announced this on Radio Pakistan and even ordered the Pakistani High Commissioner in Delhi to personally report his condition to the pilot's illustrious father—Ayub's former boss in Army HQ. On Ayub's offer to release the pilot as a goodwill gesture, the father, true to his principles, replied that all Indian POWs were his sons and in no way would he agree to only his biological son being set free. Identify the father-son duo.**

A3. Field Marshall K.M. Cariappa and Air Marshal K.C. Kariappa.

**Q4. With a long experience of operating behind enemy lines in World War II in Burma, Maj. Megh Singh of 3 Guards sensed his opportunity as Operation Gibraltar ravaged Kashmir. The army commander gave him permission to lead an unofficial, secret, irregular force of his choice and promised a promotion if he was successful. He and his force made three key raids from 1 to 11 September. What was this force, named after its leader, called? What did this force grow into on 1 July 1966 under Lt Col Megh Singh, the oldest 'ghost' unit of its kind in India?**

A4. Meghdoot Force. It grew into 9 Para SF and was called the 'ghost regiment'—it was India's first official special forces unit. The unit was divided on 1 June 1967 to form the 10 Para SF (Desert Scorpions), specialized for desert ops 9 and 10 Para SF would remain India's oldest special forces units. Lt Col Megh Singh would later raise a Border Security Force (BSF) battalion and retire as DIG.

**Q5. Which naval operation was carried out during the Kargil War to restrict Pakistani naval assets off the coast of Karachi?**

A5. Operation Talwar. While the IAF and the army's involvement in the Kargil War is well-known, the actions of the navy remain largely unknown and uncelebrated. The navy, unencumbered by the constraint of not crossing the LoC, deployed both the Western and Eastern Fleet proactively on the Arabian Sea to act as a deterrent against the Pakistan Navy as well as guard offshore assets such as Bombay High and those off the coast of Gujarat. About thirty naval warships were off the coast of Karachi and the Pakistani military leadership issued direct orders not to engage the navy.

**Q6. Which operation, conducted in 1986 by the Indian Armed Forces, involved the largest land operation since World War II?**

A6. Operation Brasstacks. A series of exercises to simulate the operational capabilities of the Indian Army, it saw the involvement of about 6,00,000 troops mobilized along the international boundary of Rajasthan. The core objective was to test new concepts of mechanization, mobility and air support. Leading this operation from the forefront was General Sundarji, the COAS. The scale of the exercise was bigger than that of any conducted by NATO—more than 10,000 armoured vehicles were spread across the Thar desert in the winter of 1986. The legacy of this exercise was that Pakistan's President Zia-ul-Haq visited India under the excuse of watching a cricket match to defuse tensions. Cricket diplomacy became regular for the two nations as India and Pakistan hosted the 1987 Cricket World Cup jointly after this.

**Q7. During the Kutch operations in 1965, the loss of access to Kanjarkot in the Great Rann led to the authorization of an Indian Army operation to retake it by force. What was this aborted operation aptly titled, considering it was a 'pursuit' in response to a Pakistani 'super raid'?**

A7. Operation Kabaddi. Capt. Sharma of 2 Sikh LI had earlier found a pot of rare Ghaznavid coins near Kanjarkot, which was later requisitioned by G3 (intel) of the 31 Infantry Brigade and delivered to Air Marshal Arjan Singh in Bhuj on his request.

**Q8. Which 'gold-strung' operation was launched by the Indian Army in 2019?**

A8. Operation Zafran. On 14 February 2019, forty Central Reserve Police Force (CRPF) personnel were martyred in Pulwama by the act of Adil Ahmed Dar, a vehicle-borne suicide bomber. Jaish-e-Mohammed claimed responsibility for the attack. India-Pakistan ties worsened following this and led to a standoff in 2019. The Indian Army moved a lot of its artillery and mechanized infantry units into the Valley to shore up its defences. The DG, Military Operations, dubbed this 'Operation Zafran' since Pulwama was a major saffron-producing area.

**Q9. The marshy haunt of scorpions, vipers and flamingos but with a seabed mineral hoard, Sir Creek is a tidal estuary that remains the sole remnant of a contested border dispute going back to 1908, when a maharaja legally sparred with the British government at Sindh. Which is this contested region that flared up in February 1965, when Pakistan captured the border fort of Kanjarkot? What happened in 2008 that led to the creation of an elite CRPF unit to prevent Pakistani infiltration through it?**

A9. The Rann of Kutch dispute. The 26/11 attacks involved the use of a route just north of the opening of Sir Creek. This led to the creation of the Creek Crocodile Commando, a special CRPF unit that was raised to protect Sir Creek.

**Did You Know?**

Thomas Henderson Brooks, an Anglo-Indian lad from Burma, is the only Indian Army general to have played in Wimbledon! He lost to Hungarian ace G. Mako in the 1938 Wimbledon championships.

**Q10. The post at Longewala was commanded by Maj. (later Brig. and Mahavir Chakra awardee) Kuldip Singh Chandpuri. Which unit did he belong to?**

Punjab Regiment insignia

A10: He was the company commander of Alpha Company of 23 Punjab. The events of the defence of Longewala have been etched into a generation's minds through the film *Border* (1997). Sunny Deol essayed the role of Maj. Chandpuri. The Punjab Regiment is one of the oldest regiments and interestingly features a naval galley as its insignia. The 23rd Battalion, however, had been raised just five years previously, on 1 October 1966.

**Q11. Over June and July 1965, Pakistan trained 6000–8000 irregular forces (mujahids), mostly radicalized youths from PoK who were given two to three weeks of training in guerrilla warfare. They were divided into ten columns of five companies each. Each column was led by PoK Army officers, supported by artillery and commandos. What were these ten columns named after in tune with standard religious optics? Which was the only column that partially succeeded in its operations while being led by a former INA officer, which would lead to Ayub Khan calling him the 'King of Rajouri'?**

A11. The columns/forces were named after famous Muslim conquerors like Babur, Tariq, Sikandar, Salahuddin, Khilji, etc. The Ghaznavi force, deployed in the Mendhar–Rajouri sector, was the only one that was partially successful. Maj. Munawar Khan Awan, who led the force, had formerly led the 2nd INA battalion in the Battle of Imphal against the British Army.

**Q12. The 11th Infantry Division, led by Maj. Gen. N.C. Rawlley (future VCOAS), was tasked with dislodging enemy mujahids who had occupied border**

**villages in the Barmer sector after the 23 September 1965 ceasefire. Gen. Rawlley was inspired by a famous World War II mobile corps to come up with a new tactic of setting up three ad hoc composite forces by mixing three different battalions, which would function as a mobile desert safari. Which famous World War II general's corps-level tactics was he trying to emulate, albeit with mixed results?**

A12. Gen. Erwin Rommel and his Afrika Corps in North Africa. This tactic would pay dividends in the Battle of Mialjar on 16 November 1965, when a composite force called the 'Sangram Force' captured the strategic village of Mialjar. Rawlley won a Military Cross during the Battle of Kohima, helped accept the Japanese surrender in British Malaya and at various points, commanded the 11th Brigade, 11th Division and 11th Corps.

**Q13. Operation Smokey (called the Battle of Hill) was a 120 Brigade operation under Brig. B.S. Ahluwalia, launched to smoke out the Pakistani unit holding Chhu-e-naar, a key hilly feature in Poonch known for its difficult geography. 2 Dogra, led by Capt. Gautam Mubayi (MVC posthumous) and N.K. Darshan Singh (MVC posthumous) suffered massive casualties but remained steadfast until, in a brilliant tactical manoeuvre reminiscent of Hrithik Roshan in *Lakshya*, 5 Sikh Light Infantry took the post. Who was the famous 5 SLI CO who was awarded the MVC**

**for this feat and would go on to receive his MVC and bar in 1971, also fondly called 'Brigadier Babaji' by his Mukti Bahini trainees?**

A13. Lt Col Sant Singh (later Brig. Sant Singh), one of only six officers (till 2022) to have won the MVC twice.

**Q14. On 5 August 1965, two nomadic porters, Mohammad Din and Wazir Mohammad from Mendhar, reported some mujahids' presence across the border to the police. This would make the SP of Baramulla rush to the HQ of the 19th Infantry Division nearby and ensure a rapid response against the infiltrators. Thus, time and again, these nomadic hill folk would be the eyes and ears of the Indian Army, providing valuable actionable intelligence in this war, as in Kargil in 1999. Which nomadic Kashmiri Gurjar pastoralist community is being talked about, with their distinctive language, culture and dress?**

A14. The Bakarwals.

**Q15. During the 1965 operations, the battle to capture the Hajipir Pass was a tough one. 19 Punjab, under Lt Col Sampuran Singh, took the steep feature of Bedori, while 1 Para CO Maj. Dayal had a close shave as three bullets were miraculously stopped by his belt. By 10 September, the historic Uri–Poonch link-up was finally completed and 19 Punjab took the important**

**feature of Kahuta on 11 September, thus closing all infiltration routes. With the massive loss of Hajipir on 29 August, a change of leadership took place in the Pakistan Army and a new Ayub Khan favourite was given brigade command. Who was this brigadier, largely known to us from his actions later in 1971?**

A15. Brig. (later Lt Gen.) A.A.K. Niazi, the man who signed the instrument of surrender in 1971. The belt containing the bullets of Maj. Dayal is displayed at the 1 Para mess. He was awarded the MVC for Hajipir and retired as Lt Gen. GOC-in-C Southern Command. Niazi was later awarded the Hilal-e-Juraat for his fictional operations in Chawinda (later shown to be false).

**Q16. One of the most archaeologically important towns of Jammu and Kashmir, it was a prominent Buddhist site in the post-Maurya, Kushana as well as Gupta eras, lying on the Silk Route branch from Taxila. It is said that Jehangir's eyesight was restored due to the cool winds of the Chenab near this town, due to which he named it the 'light of the eyes' in Persian. Identify this strategic town.**

A16. Akhnoor (from *aankh-e-noor*, with *aankh* meaning 'eyes' and *noor* meaning 'light'). Hanging like a dagger or a chicken's neck from the Jammu and Kashmir map, it is key to the supply routes to Poonch, Rajouri, Chhamb-

Jaurian and Naushera towns. In 1965, it had the only bridge across the Chenab for tanks to move through.

**Q17. At the crack of dawn on 11 September 1965, two tank regiments (4 Horse, 17 Horse), with the 16th Cavalry as flank protection and the 62nd Cavalry as a reserve, embarked on a blitzkrieg to capture Phillaura. In the resulting battle, for the loss of six Indian Centurion tanks, Pakistan would lose sixty-six and Phillaura would be historically captured by 1530 hours. This would lead the international press to term Phillaura as the '________' for the ______'. Supplied by the Americans to the Pakistan Army, the latter blank was then the most advanced tank in the world, whose invincibility would be crushed by Indian tanks, just as French invincibility was squashed in the nineteenth-century battle (the former blank). Fill in the blanks for the sensational headline.**

A17. 'Waterloo for the Patton Tanks'.

**Q18. The US had gifted Pakistan the RB 57F, a unique (only one built) modified version of the B-57 with an enormous wingspan and two auxiliary jet engines that could fly at 65,000 ft and above, well above the flight ceiling of even modern fighters. Its principal role was photo reconnaissance. One such operation was flown over Ambala on 10 October**

**1965 by Sqn Ldr Rasheed Meer, but unknown to the Pakistan Air Force, the IAF had a trump card in the form of a newly procured air defence missile. This missile had taken out a similarly invincible aircraft, launched from Peshawar five years earlier towards another target. This time, the RB 57F was hit and forced to crash land on its home base. What was this air defence missile and the famous aircraft that it shot down five years prior to the incident in question?**

A18. The S-75 Dvina (NATO name: SA-2 Guideline). It was a Soviet-designed, high-altitude air defence system. It took out the U2 aircraft being flown by Gary Powers in 1960 over Yekaterinburg. The Americans used the Peshawar air base for U2 operations and Gary Powers had also launched from there. The Hollywood movie *Bridge of Spies* was made on events related to this incident.

**Q19. It's said that this so-called champion of democracy stood disapprovingly frowning for the photo and agreed to shake hands with Lal Bahadur Shastri (LBS) only on Ayub Khan's insistence. This was so due to the lack of a mention of the Kashmir resolution in the final text. His tactic of standing precisely behind LBS has also been interpreted by some as a subconscious need to be seen dominating over the short PM Shastri—nicknamed**

**the 'Pocket Napoleon' by Americans after Tashkent. Identify this petulant person and the occasion.**

Tashkent Declaration

A19. Zulfikar Ali Bhutto, at the Tashkent Declaration. The primary mediator behind the declaration was Aleksey Kosygin (in the photo to the right of Ayub), the Soviet premier and long-standing Brezhnev rival. The Tashkent text particularly thanks him as well as the Uzbekistan government for mediation.

**Did You Know?**

The specific colour used by the IAF across aircrafts is called Tipnis Grey after Air Chief Marshal Tipnis.

**Q20. The village of Barki in Pakistan was captured by 4 Sikh regiment on 10 September 1965. However, in the subsequent task, some officers and men were taken POWs during the special operation to take**

**Khem Kharan. Six officers of 4 Sikh were moved to the fortress prison of Dargai in the Khanki valley of the North-West Frontier Province, once built by Maharaja Ranjit Singh. Why was this chosen location coincidentally apt, considering the rich regimental history that motivated the 4 Sikh officers to bear with their brutal conditions?**

A20. The Battle of Saragarhi occurred at the Saragarhi hill post just overlooking the Dargai valley. 4 Sikh is the legendary unit that took part in the battle, in which twenty-one Sikhs fought against Afridi and Orakzai tribesmen numbering 10,000 to 20,000 in 1897.

**Q21. In 1948, during the Kashmir conflict, the army commander, Gen. Harbaksh Singh, authorized 'Operation XXXXXX' in order to close the main infiltration routes. The commanding officer of the 68th Infantry Brigade under the 19th Infantry Division after whom the operation was named, was given the task of securing the key mountainous pass from the west in a pincer movement. This pass, the Hajipir Pass, was the sole connecting link between Uri and Poonch and is named after a local Sufi saint. It became the site of a bloody battle. Who was this commander?**

A21. Brig. Bakshi. An amazing adventurer, he was the first to receive the MacGregor Medal post-Independence in 1949 for his solo expedition in reconnaissance of Tibetan land routes. His VrC, won during the 1947–48 war as CO of a Gurkha unit; MVC, won as part of the Hajipir operation; VSM, won in UN Peacekeeping Force operations in the Congo; and AVSM, won in 1971, made him the 'most field decorated Indian Army general'. He retired as Lt Gen. Zorawar 'Zoru' Chand Bakshi.

**Q22. Ratanjiba was a Parsi general who was rewarded with a *jagir* of 100 villages in the district of Tarapur by Shivaji in return for his military assistance. More than three centuries later, his legendary descendant, with his name reflecting his ancestral origin, would prove his mettle at the largest tank battle in the world since World War II in Chawinda near Buttur Dograndi. Initially serving the Hyderabad state, 'Adi', as he was popularly called, would rise to command his illustrious unit in his personal tank, Khushab, and would prophetically predict his own impending martyrdom from a freak artillery shell as he led from the front despite being injured. Who was this?**

A22. Lt Col Ardeshir 'Adi' Tarapore (from Tarapur, his ancestral village), CO of 17 Poona Horse. He was awarded the highest honour of PVC posthumously for leading from the front in Phillaura and Chawinda sectors. Lt Col Tarapore's tank is named after the Battle of Khushab in 1857, part of the First Anglo-Persian War where a lightning charge by the 3rd Bombay Light Cavalry (ancestral regiment of 17 Horse) extricated the force from an ambush by Persian forces, leading to 2 Victoria Crosses (British PVC equivalent).

**Q23. During the Kutch operations, in response to the capture of Kanjarkot by Pakistan, India launched a psychological warfare tactic on 26 March 1965. A joint exercise called 'Arrow Head' was executed to showcase the heavily defended crown jewel of Indian power projection by moving it to the Kutch port of Mandvi. What is being talked about?**

A23. Aircraft carrier INS *Vikrant*. Largely associated with the glory of the 1971 war, it would remain in refitting at Bombay for the entirety of the war in 1965.

**Q24. Unbeknown to most during the 1965 war, a lone, highly advanced French Alize was flown by the secretive Indian naval aviation unit INAS 310 'Cobras'. It was tasked with electronic warfare, signal interception as well as the reconnaissance of Pakistani positions on the high seas, including the tracking of submarines as well as ground locations. True to its classified nature, it was rarely seen by mainstream troops. This led to a peculiarly dangerous problem/threat that the Alize pilots got used to. What problem?**

A24. Since they had never seen it before, Indian air defence personnel mistook it for a secret Pakistani aircraft and took a shot at it. The aircraft survived and gave loads of valuable intel to the IAF during the war, which was utilized in attacking the airfields of Sargodha, Peshawar as well as the Badin radar. The INAS 310 'Cobras' unit calls its CO, aptly, 'King Cobra', with the first king cobra being Vice Admiral M.K. Roy (he was director, naval intelligence in 1971 and was responsible for the planning of Operation Jackpot).

**Q25. Four Mughal emperors (Babur, Jehangir, Shah Jahan and Alamgir), two key military leaders of Arabia (Badr and Khaibar) and a lone Tipu Sultan departed from Karachi on 7 September 1965 in an attempt at national morale-building to distract the masses from India's dangerous counter-offensive in Punjab on 6 September 1965. On paper, the target was a fictional Indian radar in this ancient city, but the real target was a famous religious and political symbol, reconstructed many times, which has polarized India since the twelfth century. Identify the city and the target, and also the name of the operation.**

A25. Operation Dwarka. The target was the bombarding of the famed Somnath Temple. No damage was done either to Somnath or to anything tangible in the city of Dwarka, yet Pakistanis celebrate 7 September as Navy Day. Many members of the operation rose to senior positions in the Pakistan Navy, including future CNS Admiral Karamat Niazi.

**Q26. Operation Dwarka had a silent protector, which kept monitoring and relaying Indian naval positions during the attack. This silent protector would be detected on 13 September by INS *Kuthar* but failed to neutralize it. Throughout the war, it would keep harassing Indian ships, leading to scares, especially in the Bombay port, where INS *Vikrant* was docked. Which was this silent protector, which was finally bested in 1971?**

A26. PNS *Ghazi*, the Pakistani submarine. India did not possess a submarine in 1965 while Pakistan had only one, PNS *Ghazi*.

**Q27. What is Establishment 22?**

A27. The Special Frontier Force (SFF), called Est 22 in reference to the first Inspector General, Maj. Gen. S.S. Uban, who had commanded the 22nd Mountain Regiment in World War II. Raised in the 1962 Sino-Indian War, with efforts from B.N. Mullick of the IB and Biju Patnaik, the future chief minister of Odisha, it recruited Tibetan exiles, especially the Khampas of Chushi Gandruk, who were highly specialized in mountain warfare. The SFF follows a different rank structure than that of the Indian Army, harking back to the hierarchy of the Tibetan forces. All recruits are imparted airborne and special forces training. They have been instrumental in a number of missions, including the mountaineering expedition to Nanda Devi led by M.S. Kohli to place a nuclear test detector to gauge China's nuclear tests in Xinjiang province.

**Q28. 1971 saw the SFF extensively man the Chittagong Hill Tracts as they imparted training to the Mukti Bahini, thus preventing another ethnicity-based genocide. This was the first time the SFF battalion was commanded by one of their own, Dapon. In which recent clash did this force decisively take part?**

A28. The 2020 Galwan skirmish. The SFF turned the tide yet again as these specialized mountaineers were instrumental in conquering vital positions in the high-altitude terrain. One SFF soldier lost his life to a landmine placed in the ridges but was instrumental in securing the land tract that allowed the Indian Army to gain the advantage of height in the difficult terrain.

**Did You Know?**

Naib Risaldar Sultana Singh was martyred in the last stand by Guides Cavalry to protect British resident Louis Cavagnari in the Siege of Kabul of 1879. Three generations later, his great-grandson would make his name against the same NFWP tribes and eventually rise to be Marshal of the Air—Arjan Singh, the only five-star IAF officer till date.

**Q29. The tasks assigned to this naval task force were the establishment of effective control of the seaward approaches, neutralizing the coast batteries defending the ports and sinking or immobilizing units of the opposition. The naval task force was divided into four task groups: the Surface Action Group comprising the Indian naval ships INS *Mysore*, INS *Trishul*, INS *Betwa*, INS *Beas* and INS *Cauvery*; the Carrier Task Group comprising ships INS *Vikrant*, INS *Delhi*, INS *Kuthar*, INS *Kirpan*, INS *Khukri* and INS *Rajput*; the Mine Sweeping Group comprising mine-sweepers INS *Karwar*, INS *Kakinada*, INS *Cannanore* and INS *Bimlipatam*; and finally, the Support Group comprising the solo ship INS *Dharini*. Which conflict was this force involved in?**

A29. The capture of Anjadiv Island was considered the primary task for the naval task force as the Portuguese provocative operations had originated on this island. The liberation was carried out by sending landing parties from INS *Trishul* and giving covering fire from INS *Trishul* and INS *Mysore*. The landing operations were successfully carried out under Lt. Arun Auditto, who was Officer-in-Charge, Naval Landing Party, and the first phase was completed at 1425 hours on 18 December 1961. In the liberation of Anjadiv Island, seven sailors laid down their lives, and two officers and seventeen sailors were wounded. A memorial was later erected at Flagstaff Point on Anjadiv Island to commemorate those sailors of the Indian Navy who made the supreme sacrifice.

**Q30. Army Day is celebrated on 15 January every year to commemorate the date when Field Marshal K.M. Cariappa took over as the first Commander-in-Chief of the Indian Army from General F.R. Bucher on 15 January 1949. However, 27 October is celebrated as Infantry Day to recognize which seminal event in the history of a newly independent India?**

A30. This date marks the occasion when the 1st Sikh Regiment made its way into Srinagar Airfield in 1947 on Dakotas of the No. 12 Squadron and heroically defended the nation against Pakistani intruders. The No. 12 Squadron of the IAF is nicknamed 'The Striking Yaks'. The first IAF squadron to be converted into a transport role, it distinguished itself under its first CO, Wg Cdr K.L. Bhatia, in the 1947–48 war, leading a humongous airlifting effort.

**Q31. The crucial airlift to Srinagar by the air force was responsible for sustained air operations in support of the Indian Army and the civilian authorities. Besides the air force, a number of private aircraft were also pressed into action. One such daredevil who piloted the air support went on to become the chief minister of an Indian state in future. Who was this?**

A31. Biju Patnaik of Orissa. One of the original Dakotas, #VP 905, was refurbished and given to the IAF later. The aircraft, now called Parashurama, now flies with the IAF Heritage Flight.

**Q32. This Indian Army officer played a key role during the Indo-Pakistani War of 1947. As the commanding officer of the 1st battalion, the Sikh Regiment (1 Sikh), he was the first recipient of the Maha Vir Chakra posthumously. 1 Sikh was the first unit to be inducted into the war, when it was airlifted from Gurgaon to Srinagar on 27 October 1947. Who was this?**

A32. Lt Col Dewan Ranjit Rai, MVC (1913–47). Under Rai's command, the battalion fought with tremendous spirit and bravery and played a key role in saving the valley of Kashmir from invaders. His citation read, 'As very little time was at his disposal, he personally conducted reconnaissance and operations at such personal risk that he was eventually killed. By his complete disregard for personal danger and his determined and inspired leadership, the raiders were stopped sufficiently far away to enable a build-up for the eventual decisive defeat. The officer gave his life in a successful endeavour to save Srinagar by displaying courage of the highest order.'

**Q33. On 11 December 2021, four veterans, Lt Gen. R.R. Goswami, Maj. Gen. S. Jaswal, Col T. Kochappan and Col P. Tembe, supported by 120 paratroopers**

**of the elite Shatrujeet airborne brigade, led a mass para jump in Agra. Dedicated to the memory of late Gen. Rawat, the fiftieth anniversary of which iconic paradrop was being commemorated?**

Tangail Paradrop

A33. The Tangail Paradrop during the 1971 operations. It was the largest airborne operation in Indian military history and one of the biggest paradrops globally after Operation Market Garden in World War II. At the Republic Day Parade of 2021, the IAF honoured the operation by recreating the 'Tangail formation' with one Dakota and two Caribous (the aircraft used in the airdrop along with An-12, Caribous, C-119).

**Q34. 2 Para battalion of 750 paratroopers led by Lt Col K.S. Pannu was airdropped in Tangail through the day of 11 December 1971. Aimed at cutting off the Paki 93rd Brigade, what was the primary objective? It is now named after Bongobondhu Mujibur Rehman and is the sixth largest of its kind in South Asia.**

A34. The Poongli Bridge. One of the most important bridges over the river Jamuna (a continuation of the Brahmaputra in its southern flow), the control of this bridge was essential to cutting off retreating Pakistani forces to defend Dhaka. Lt Col K.S. Pannu was awarded the MVC for this operation. To misdirect the Pakistani reconnaissance troops on the ground from the actual location of the drop, the IAF conducted feint drops using dummies.

**Q35. The lightning success in Tangail would enable 2 Para to achieve an eagerly awaited honour, leaving many other units behind—all of whom were engaged in competitive rivalry as a morale booster around the theatre. What was this honour, that would eventually lead to the iconic surrender of 93,000 troops?**

A35. 2 Para, in its rapid dash became the first unit to enter the crown jewel, Dhaka, on 16 December at 1042 hours. They received the initial ceasefire from Lt Gen. A.A.K. Niazi and, accompanied by the firebrand revolutionary Tiger Siddiqui, entered Pakistani Eastern Command in Dhaka to take Lt Gen. Niazi into custody. Abdul Kadir 'Tiger' Siddiqui was a legendary twenty-six-year-old guerrilla fighter who led a 17,000-strong force called the 'Tiger Bahini' in Tangail and was a key ally to Indian forces in the region.

**Q36. On the eve of the Tangail op, the DGMO asked Ramamohan Rao, an officer in the Directorate of Public Relations, to ensure good publicity of the op in the international press as 'psyops' (psychological warfare to demoralize the Pakistanis). By 12 December, Rao faced a dilemma, realizing that there were no available photos of the op. This would entail Rao coming up with a creative solution that would play a key role in convincing Niazi to surrender. What did he do?**

A36. Rao used the photo of an old Indian Army paradrop exercise in Agra as the Tangail airdrop by removing the 'file photo' title. This then was reported across the global press, including the BBC and *The Times*, as the actual Tangail photo. Interestingly, the fake photo showed a whole brigade (5000 troops) landing while actually, only a battalion strength (700 soldiers) had been deployed. The Pakistan Army thought a whole para brigade was attacking them and surrendered in panic. Rao's talent in psyops would be noticed by none other than RAW chief R.N. Kao and Rao was recruited into RAW as a 'Kaoboy'.

**Q37. After a series of name changes, the 15th Ludhiana Sikhs ultimately became the 2nd Sikh Battalion (2 Sikh) in the independent Indian Army. Which veteran from this unit handled his 'captaincy' as ADC to the**

**army commander in the 1965 war with as much elan as his later stint in politics?**

A37. Capt. Amarinder Singh, former CM of Punjab. Capt. Amarinder Singh was the ADC to GOC-in-C Western Command Lt Gen. Harbaksh Singh during the 1965 war. He has kept a dedicated room in his official house for 2nd Sikh and its heritage, including its finest hour in the capture of the Raja Post in Kashmir (1965 war) against significant odds.

**Q38. Formed in 1990 as an elite counter-insurgency force of 80,000 by reforming two corps-level formations, which force remains the only one to have a modified AK-47 assault rifle as its regimental crest?**

Rashtriya Rifles badge

A38. Rashtriya Rifles (RR). Although known largely for their operations in the Kashmir Valley, RR was first used in Punjab to battle the Khalistanis before being deployed to the Valley. They were the first regular Indian unit (other than Special Forces) to use AK-47s (best suited in urban warfare settings of cordon and search).

**Q39. The RR was one of the first regular Indian units to train with AK-47s in the 1990s while other units used the Indian Small Arms System (INSAS). There's one intriguing peculiarity about the AK-47s used by RR with respect to the origins of these guns. This peculiarity has been a source of much angst for the Soviet (later Russian) Kalashnikov company. What is this peculiarity, which still exists?**

A39. Despite having a very close relationship with the USSR (later Russia), India never bought AK-47s from them, despite the AKs being Russia's most common global defence export. For RR also, only Bulgarian AK-47 variants were bought. This continues to hold true in the Indian Army as most AK-47s are Bulgarian/Czech-sourced rather than Russian. The Indo-Russian deal of the indigenous production of AK-203 rifles may address this issue in future.

**Q40. If Counter Insurgency Force (CIF) R/Romeo Force was responsible for Rajouri and Poonch, Delta Force for Doda, Victor Force for Anantnag, Pulwama, Shopian, Kulgam and Budgam and Kilo Force for**

**Kupwara, Baramulla and Srinagar, then which region did Counter Insurgency Force (CIF) U/Uniform Force deal with?**

A40. Udhampur and Banihal. Jawans, JCOs and officers from all arms and services of the Army serve in the Rashtriya Rifles on a deputation basis, with a tenure in the RR being two to three years. The infantry provides half of the manpower (50 per cent infantry), services such as Army Service Corps (ASC), Corps of Signals, Corps of Electronics and Mechanical Engineers (EME) provide around 10 per cent and other arms provide around 40 per cent of the total strength.

**Q41. Distinctively associated with the RR uniform, this lightweight gear has a ballistic strip manufactured by Phantom steel with provision for flaps and protection from AK-47 fire at 25m and 9mm fire at 10m. Battle-tested and long known for its ergonomic efficiency, it is gradually being replaced by the modern MKU ballistic helmets. What was this iconic headgear that might remind you of the Maratha empire flag?**

Patka helmet

A41. The Patka helmets. A Zari Patka is one of the flags that the Marathas had, which was mostly used for ceremonial purposes. It had a saffron swallow-tailed flag, which had a zari border at its edges; there was another flag which was the plain bhagava flag, so sometimes both the flags were flown. In addition to these, each of the Maratha chiefs had their own flags; the Sindhias had the sun in the centre with two snakes on the side on a saffron background and so on.

**Q42. A Kashmiri carpet weaver by profession, this Wani clan member became a counter-insurgent after seeing the futility of violence in the 1990s. Working his way through Ikhwan and then Jammu and Kashmir Light Infantry (JAKLI), he would become a legend in RR, winning the Sena Medal twice before being martyred in Op Batagund in 2018 while neutralizing LeT terrorists. Identify this Kulgam RR icon, the first man from the Kashmir Valley to be awarded the Ashok Chakra.**

Lance Naik Ahmad Wani

A42. Lance Naik Ahmad Wani. He started his career as a part of Ikhwan, a pro-government anti-terror militia helmed by Kuka Parray. Parray's assassination in 2003 in Bandipora was termed by Mufti Mohammad as a huge setback to the peace process. Ikhwan was disbanded and many of its former members joined the Indian defence forces, especially JAKLI, Kashmir state police and RR. Initially a part of the 162nd TA, Wani was deputed to RR from JAKLI.

**Q43. The erstwhile maharaja of Jaipur, this legendary soldier and MVC awardee began his career in the President's Bodyguard before his SF career. A successful diplomat as well as a businessman, he would famously be called out of retirement by Rajiv Gandhi to boost the morale of his unit after the debacle in Op Pawan in Sri Lanka. He would eventually achieve a rare honour. Who was this, and which honour?**

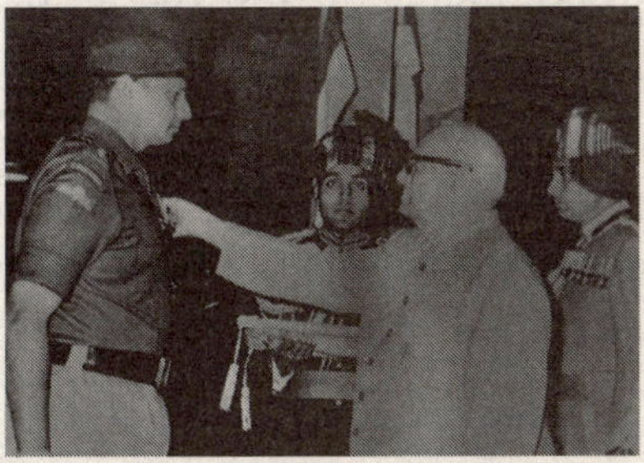

Brig. (then Lt Col) Sawai Bhawani Singh being presented the Maha Vir Chakra by President V.V. Giri

A43. Brig. Maharaja Sawai Bhawani Singh MVC, and the honour was a promotion after retirement. He retired from the Indian Army as a colonel but was made an honorary brigadier for his actions in boosting his unit's morale after their loss in the Jaffna helidrop.

**Q44. In the wake of the 1965 War, Meghdoot Force under Lt Col Megh Singh formed the first SF unit, 9 Para SF, in 1966. On 1 June 1967, 9 Para was divided into two battalions, with 10 Para coming into existence at Gwalior under its first CO, Lt Col N.S. Uttaiah. Under the command of Lt Col Bhawani Singh from 19 August 1968, 10 Para would be based out of Nasirabad, Rajasthan. Quite suited to their operational specialization in the Thar, what would they be eventually known as?**

A44. 'Desert Scorpions'. The basic sub-unit of 10 Para was a squad consisting of six troopers under a squad commander. Four squads formed a team and three teams an assault group. Each squad was self-sufficient to operate alone and each commando acquired two main skills in demolition, comms, medical or driving. Three assault groups—Alpha, Bravo and Charlie—were formed in 1968.

**Q45. Known as one of the most daring raids in the history of Indian special ops, which raid did 10 Para SF**

**execute on 7 December 1971 in the deserts of Sindh, deep behind enemy lines (80 km from IB)?**

10 Para in action

A45. The Chachro Raid. 10 Para was tasked to raid Chachro, the Wing HQ of Pakistani Rangers deployed in Tharparkar, and disrupt the line of communications along the Chachro-Umarkot axis. Inspired by the British SAS raid behind enemy lines at a German airfield in Fuka, Libya, during the Second World War, this successful operation established the Indian Army's dominance in the desert during the 1971 war. For four days, the battalion infiltrated deep inside enemy territory and carried out raids on enemy positions at Chachro and Virwah. Umarkot, incidentally, was the birthplace of Akbar and the first princely state to willingly accede to Pakistan.

**Q46. The main problem 10 Para faced during the planning of the Chachro Raid was the lack of maps of the region, especially of navigable roads or tracks. This needed local tracking experts. What creative solution was found?**

A46. They made contact with Thakur Balwant Singh, a dacoit who ran a smuggling racket along Barmer, Gujarat and Sindh. He sent a strong contingent of Khoja tribals (Barwariya Rajputs), who knew the terrain very well.

**Q47. In its thirty-two-year history of counter-insurgency, RR has lost a CO (of colonel rank) only twice, both times of the 21st battalion. In 2000, in a tragic incident, Brig. B.S. Shergill and Col Rajinder Chauhan were martyred by a triggered blast near Handwara. This is probably one of the earliest examples of the use of what, which has become the USP of modern-day terror?**

Brig. B.S. Shergill and Col R. Chauhan

A47. IED (improvised explosive device). An IED was planted on the route that was being used by the army convoy. It was blown up as the convoy passed by. Col Ashutosh Sharma, CO 21 RR, was martyred in 2020 while leading a CASO. He is one of the few soldiers (probably the only soldier) in the Indian Army to have won the Sena Medal thrice (third time posthumously), with Maj. Anuj Sood receiving the Shaurya Chakra.

**Did You Know?**

The Victoria Memorial in Kolkata was painted black with a mixture of mud and dung to make it inconspicuous from Japanese air raids during World War II.

# Section 4

## The Operations, Warriors, Traditions and Colours of the Men in Uniform

Other than fighting wars and protecting the nation, the proud men in uniform have excelled in fields as varied as Bollywood and politics. While some have gone on to author books, others have written inspirational songs. They have served humanity not only in India but as part of humanitarian and disaster relief efforts across the world. Then there is the case of families where successive generations have served in uniform and multiple family members have been part of a rich tradition of various regiments and battalions, each shining brighter than the other. Men of British origin, born in India and serving in the Indian Army, have conducted research that led to the discovery of new lands, Nobel Prize-winning research and other such mind-boggling endeavours. In a world where a person of Indian origin has become the prime minister of the UK, this association seems especially relevant. This section delves into hidden gems about the personae that have been forgotten by time and the world but whose contributions to our society and daily living remain unmatched. That a number of them were associated with the armed forces during their lives is a matter of pride for us and should be celebrated by one and all. It is our endeavour to give the reader a taste of some of what lies undiscovered and unknown.

**Q1. Operation Polo in 1948 was quite an international affair. The Nizam of Hyderabad's army consisted of mercenary Pathans from Afghanistan, led by an Egyptian general, El Edroos. He was supported by a nascent Pakistan, obtained armaments from the UK and was being given tacit support by another European nation. Which nation?**

A1. Portugal. Fearing a similar action in Goa, the Portuguese supported the Nizam in his endeavours to avoid joining India. Op Polo lasted five days and resulted in the accession of Hyderabad to the Union of India.

**Q2: What was the name of the humanitarian assistance activity launched by the Ministry of External Affairs in 2017 to help Bangladesh during the Rohingya crisis?**

A2: Operation Insaniyat. A military crackdown in the Rakhine state of Myanmar saw around 3,79,000 Rohingya Muslims flee Myanmar into Bangladesh. Two consignments of food materials, infant food formula, rainwear as well as mosquito nets were delivered to the port city of Chittagong. India also declared $25 million as development assistance for Rakhine state in December 2017.

**Q3: What operation by the Indian Air Force in 2016 was launched to address the crisis in Juba, South Sudan?**

A3: Operation Sankat Mochan. Against the backdrop of the South Sudanese civil war, rival factions loyal to President Salva Kiir and Vice President Riek Machar initiated clashes in the capital city in July 2016. Three hundred people, including many civilians, were killed in the clash, with many fighting areas located next to UN bases. Two C-17 Globemasters were deployed to evacuate 600 Indians as well as foreign nationals.

**Q4: What friendly name was given to the humanitarian assistance and disaster relief operation for the Nepal earthquake in 2015?**

A4: Operation Maitri. The day of 25 April 2015 witnessed Nepal being rocked by an earthquake with a magnitude of 7.8. It killed a total of 8900 people in Nepal and triggered an avalanche on Mt Everest that killed seventeen. India was the first responder, with a multifaceted team consisting of the NDRF, IAF, medical teams and engineer task forces.

**Q5: What relief operation carried out in Uttarakhand in 2013 involved the IAF airlifting 19,600 people to safety?**

A5: Operation Rahat. On 16 June 2013, a mid-day cloudburst over Uttarakhand caused landslides and floods that affected more than 30,000 pilgrims. It also flooded the Kedarnath temple and melted the Kedarnath mountain. More than 5500 people were lost and assumed dead. The IAF deployed huge air resources for search and rescue, evacuation and rehabilitation. Over 2000 sorties were flown and 3,82,400 kg of equipment and material were dropped for the operation.

**Q6: By what name were the air efforts of the Kargil War known?**

A6: Operation Safed Sagar. The high degree of imagination and flexibility that was displayed by the IAF to coordinate its attacks with the forces on the ground led to the integral disruption of supplies of the enemy at Muntho Dhalo. The enemy's command and control were left in disarray owing to precise strikes at the Battalion HQ of Tiger Hill, allowing the army to overrun the fortified defences of the enemy.

**Q7: Which prickly operation foiled the coup on the Maldives government in 1988?**

A7: Operation Cactus. The day of 3 November 1988 saw the island nation of Maldives besieged by a coup. The Indian response was spearheaded by the 50 Independent Para Brigade under the leadership of Brig. Farrokh Bulsara with air and naval support provided by the 44 Squadron and INS *Betwa* and *Godavari*. With flawless execution, Col S.C. Joshi and Maj. R.J.S. Dhillon secured the Maldivian president from his house and all rebels and coup leaders were rounded up. Within two weeks, order was restored and the Indian Army was de-inducted on 17 November.

**Q8: Which operation involved a relief package flown into Jaffna by the IAF in 1987?**

A8: Operation Poomalai, which translates to 'flower garland'. The Sinhalese government had put restrictive measures on supplies to the north and the east of their country, controlled by Tamil rebels. An-32s were loaded with supplies and 23 tonnes of relief material were airdropped into Sri Lanka by the IAF.

**Q9: Which operation by the Indian Army was named after a poem by Kalidasa and involved training in Antarctica?**

A9: Operation Meghdoot. Launched on 13 April 1984, Vaisakhi day, it pre-empted Pakistan's Operation Ababeel to take control of the Siachen glacier. A cartographer named Hodgson in the US, while charting maps for the USAF, had drawn a line on the map that, if accepted by the international community, would have given the region of the Siachen glacier to Pakistan.

Col Narendra 'Bull' Kumar designed and executed a plan that involved the acclimatization of a number of troops, including an expedition to Antarctica in 1982. A full battalion of the Kumaon Regiment and a unit of Ladakh Scouts acquired the Siachen glacier for India after an incredibly tough climb.

**Q10. What was the name of the operation that saw the Indian Army capture the highest battle post on Siachen?**

A10: Operation Rajiv. In 1987, the Pakistan Army infiltrated the Siachen area and occupied the highest position, which they had dubbed Quaid Post after Quaid-E-Azam, Jinnah. An effort by a JAKLI patrol led by 2/Lt Rajiv Pande to conquer this impenetrable ice fortress led to his demise along with that of ten other soldiers. After a couple of setbacks, a five-member team led by Naib Subedar Bana Singh conquered the icy climb and captured the post. The post was later renamed 'Bana Top' and Naib Subedar (now Honorary Captain) Bana Singh was awarded the Param Vir Chakra, one of the only three living recipients of the award.

**Did You Know?**

The Sea King Mark (Mk) 42 Anti-Submarine Warfare helicopters are nicknamed 'harpoons' as their role in detecting submarines is akin to the usage of a harpoon, a long spear-like instrument used in fishing, whaling, sealing and other marine mammal hunting.

**Q11: Which operation was launched by the Indian Navy for the flood-affected state of Kerala in 2018?**

A11: Operation Madad. This was launched on 9 August 2018 by the Southern Naval Command in the wake of the incessant rainfall and release of excess water from Idukki and other dams. Multiple diving teams, the INHS *Sanjivani* and INS *Venduruthy* were involved in the relief ops. The floods were the worst the state had seen in a century, with 445 dead and fifteen missing; the loss of life, limb and property was to haunt the state for years to come.

**Q12: Which rescue operation was carried out in 2018 by the navy on the Yemeni island of Socotra?**

A12: Operation Raahat. The severe cyclonic storm Mekenu crossed the Yemeni island of Socotra on 24 May 2018. It sank and damaged three Indian dhows at harbour while another, MSV *Safina* with twelve aboard, was reported to be missing. The navy undertook two aerial sorties on 27 and 28 May 2018 to search for the missing Indians. INS *Sunayna* was called into service to rescue the stranded individuals from the island of Socotra.

**Q13. A major tradition exists in India wherein families have served the nation in the defence forces with distinction across generations. Many stories of such**

**families can be found. One such unique family was that of the Vohras. The eldest brother was commissioned in 1942. The youngest brother retired in 1996. During this span, the four brothers collectively served the nation for 150 years! The Vohra family is unique, with four real brothers joining the army. Of the four, two rose to the rank of lieutenant general and two became major generals. All four served in the same corps. Which one?**

A13. Armoured Corps. Inder Mohan Vohra got his commission in 1942 and joined the 8th Cavalry Regiment. Jagat Mohan Vohra got commissioned into the Deccan Horse. Raj Mohan Vohra was commissioned in 1952, into the Scinde Horse (14 Horse). Satish Mohan Vohra was with the 3rd Cavalry. Both Inder Mohan and Raj commanded the Army War College. Jagat and Raj also commanded the same armoured division. A third coincidence is that Jagat led the same armoured brigade that his eldest brother had raised into the 1971 war.

**Q14. A test pilot and an aircraft designer, this German designed aircraft for the Luftwaffe, including Fw190 and Ta152. The latter was given the 'Ta' prefix to honour his work by the German Air Ministry. Post-World War II, he worked in India, had A.P.J. Abdul Kalam as one of his students and helped design the Marut HF-24, the first indigenous fighter bomber. Who was this?**

Kurt Tank

A14. Kurt Tank. The first prototype of the Marut HF-24 flew in 1961 and retired from active service in 1985. Tank had been, appropriately, a highly decorated cavalry officer during the First World War. India presented an HF-24 to Germany in March 1985 to the Deutsche Museum in Munich in acknowledgement of Dr Kurt Tank's leadership.

**Q15. After the ceasefire over Kutch operations in 1965, British PM Harold Wilson offered to mediate in the conflict that ultimately led to the Kutch agreement on 1 July. As per the deal, the dispute was referred to a UN arbitration tribunal which, on 19 February 1968, gave its verdict, which was accepted by both sides. To maintain the neutrality of the tribunal, India, Pakistan and the UN Secretary-General nominated one member each to the panel. Who was the Pakistan nominee, a darling of the west as well as the Shah of Iran, who, till date, is the only Iranian to have been the UN General Assembly (UNGA) president (1950)?**

A15. Nasrollah Entezam. The two other tribunal members were Ales Bebler (a Yugoslavian judge nominated by India) and Gunnar Lagersen (a Swedish judge nominated by U Thant, Secretary-General, the UN). It remains and shall probably remain the only Indo-Pak dispute successfully solved by international arbitration. Since the Shimla agreement of 1972, it is mandated that any Indo-Pak conflicts in the future have to be resolved bilaterally.

**Q16. In 2011, a retired F-86 sabre pilot, Qaiser Hussain, wrote to Farida Singh, daughter of Jehangir 'Jungoo' Engineer, apologizing for his action on 19 September 1965 of shooting down an aircraft supposedly doing reconnaissance of the Kutch border for India to open a new front in the conflict. Why did the Pakistani fighter pilot apologize sixty-five years later for his actions, which caused major controversy?**

A16. The aircraft was an unarmed Beechcraft and was not a military aircraft. It was carrying the CM of Gujarat, Balwant Rai Mehta, his wife, three members of his staff, two journalists and two crew, all of whom were tragically killed. He was travelling from Bhuj to the Tata Chemicals factory in Mithapur and got lost en route. B.R. Mehta gained fame for the B.R. Mehta commission that brought the Panchayati Raj concept to India. The Beechcraft pilot was former IAF pilot Jehangir Engineer, one of the four legendary Engineer brothers—Aspy became Air Chief, Minoo became AOC-in-C

Western Air Command during 1971 while Ronnie took sudden retirement as Gp Capt. in 1967 to migrate to Canada after an illustrious IAF career. All three had been awarded DFCs in World War II. Jungoo became a famous figure in civil aviation and VVIP transport after retiring from the IAF.

**Q17. Sukarno, the president of Indonesia from 1945 to 1967, had a significant bonhomie with US allies in South Asia, especially Pakistan, with whom he had signed a mutual defence agreement. In September 1965, Sukarno stunningly offered the visiting Pakistani ambassador aid in an ambitious naval venture using patrol ships and aerial reconnaissance jets, which would catch India unawares in a territory distant from its mainland. What was this far-fetched Indonesian offer?**

A17. An offer to annex the Andaman and Nicobar Islands for Pakistan. Sukarno's name was derived from the Mahabharata hero Karna. It was this same person who was helped by Biju Patnaik (future CM of Orissa) while he was fighting the Dutch for the independence of Indonesia in 1947. In fact, Sukarno named his daughter Megawati at the suggestion of Biju Patnaik. She went on to become the president of Indonesia. So much for gratitude!

**Q18. He spearheaded the manufacture of the first IAF aircraft, called Kanpur I and Kanpur II. In what**

**is undoubtedly extremely rare in the Indian armed forces, this man started off as a *hawai* sepoy in 1932 and rose to become an air vice marshal in the IAF. The first AOC-in-C of Maintenance Command in 1955, he was a legendary engineer, having been made an MBE (Member of the British Empire) as a flying officer in 1943. Who was this?**

A18. AVM Harjinder Singh VSM Class I (now called PVSM) MBE. Much before *atmanirbhar* was introduced to our vocabulary, he had demonstrated the same at Kanpur. He had incredible successes during World War II in ensuring aircraft serviceability, often with very little or no resources at his command. A large area in Kanpur is named Harjinder Nagar after him.

**Q19. A distinguished Zoroastrian family, it had four sons in the IAF. One went on to become the chief of air staff. Another became an air marshal. Three won the DFC. The fourth went on to head Ops, Planning and Training for Indian Airlines. Which family is this?**

The Engineers

A19. The Engineer family. Aspy Engineer won the DFC and was made the CAS when Subroto Mukherjee passed away. Minoo Engineer remains to date the most decorated officer in the IAF. A DFC during World War II, MVC for Ops in Jammu and Kashmir, PVSM for his role in 1962 support ops and finally a Padma Bhushan as AOC-in-C WAC during the 1971 Indo-Pak war. Rohinton Engineer also won the DFC and fought during the 1965 war. Jehangir Engineer was the fourth.

**Q20. In 1997, she was decommissioned with the last signal by Cdr H.S. Rawat, captain of the ship, which read:**

**'In a few hours from now, I will come to rest**
**But in these 36 years, I think I did my best**
**For my fleet and navy I earned great name**
**That's why they call me "Lady of Khulna" fame**
**With admin and ops support coming from you**
**And the fine skills of the dockyard too**
**The Western Fleet, the best in the side**
**Serving for you all, we did with the pride**
**Now I am going, I bid adieu**
**And with all good wishes coming from you**
**Though I will be striking down the pennant from main**
**I do hope XXXXXXX will be with you soon again.'**
**Who was the Lady of Khulna?**

A20. INS *Vikrant* (1961–97). Initially called the Hercules, she was the Indian Navy's first aircraft carrier with British Sea Hawks and Alizé anti-submarine aircraft, later fielding HAL Chetaks and Seakings as well. She was instrumental in the naval blockade of East Pakistan and the bombing of Chittagong and Khulna to cripple the forces and deter a naval thrust in that axis, earning her crew two MVC and twelve VrC. *The Lady* returned as INS *Vikrant*, which was commissioned on 2 September 2022, as India became the sixth nation to indigenously build an aircraft carrier, an exclusive club!

**Did You Know?**

In 1948, Prithi and Kushal Chand, a duo of Lahauli brothers, led a voluntary detachment that created artificial avalanches by beating kettles and drums to cross the ice-laden Zojila Pass. Zojila Pass is one of the only two gateways from Kashmir via Sonmarg to Ladakh. Till then, no mountaineer had ever crossed Zojila during the winters and this action saved Leh from certain fall to Pakistan. Also they remain the only two brothers to have been awarded the Maha Vir Chakra.

**Q21: *A Bridge Too Far* is a 1974 book by Cornelius Ryan about the failed Allied operation Market Garden. This was later adapted into a 1977 movie by**

**Richard Attenborough. But who authored the book *A Ridge Too Far*?**

A21: Capt. Amarinder Singh, the past CM of Punjab, who held the chair on two occasions! Born into the royal family of Patiala, he attended the NDA and was commissioned into the Sikh Regiment in 1963. He served as aide-de-camp to Lt Gen. Harbaksh Singh, the western army commander. He saw active service in the 1965 war but retired in 1966. He authored this book. which details the experiences of the Indian Infantry in the Kargil War as they put up a fitting riposte to the Pakistan Army when they strayed 'a ridge too far'.

**Q22. How did the name of an Indian actress adorn a bomb meant for the Pakistani Prime Minister Nawaz Sharif?**

Raveena Tandon bomb

A22: It's been a long-drawn taunt between the countries of India and Pakistan where often, the Pakistani raiders and even the regular army would taunt their Indian counterparts. They would haughtily agree to give up their posts and even Lahore for the likes of Madhuri Dixit or Raveena Tandon, who ruled the silver screens in the 1990s. Pakistani PM Nawaz Sharif was one such fan of Raveena. When the armies met in Tololing of Drass sector, the taunts continued and rose to prominence, especially as the Pakistan Army, marauding as a band of muhajirs, captured Tiger Hill. As a fitting reply, the IAF, in its Operation Safed Sagar, cheekily chalked out a special message for the enemy PM himself.

**Q23. The principal international personalities involved were Hammarskjold, Kasavubu, Lumumba and Tshombe. On the Indian side, it was Wg Cdr A.I.K. Suares who led the No. 5 squadron, the Tuskers, flying Canberras into the thick of the chaotic action. His commander was a Canadian Royal Air Force officer. This was October 1961. Where was this action taking place?**

A23. The Congo. This was in the aftermath of the sudden and violent end of the Belgian rule over the Congo that quickly descended into a civil war. The United Nations stepped in and the IAF sent its aircraft to support this mission. The UN air effort was a mixed bag of six F-86 Sabre fighters from the Ethiopian Air Force, six Saab

J 29s of the Royal Swedish Air Force, a full squadron of sixteen Fairchild C-119 transports from the Italian Air Force and a combined UN Dakota squadron crewed by members of various air forces, including those of Argentina and Brazil, and commanded by Wg Cdr G.B. Singh of the Indian Air Force.

**Q24. One of only six officers to have won the Maha Vir Chakra twice, this Chennai-born pilot won a Vayu Sena Medal (VM) for his exploits in the Congo before being awarded an MVC in the 1965 and 1971 war each. Who was this brilliant pilot, who unfortunately died in an air crash in 1972?**

A24. Wg Cdr Padmanabha Gautam. He undertook six important offensive and tactical close-support operations over Pakistani territory during the period between 6 and 21 September 1965. These missions included reconnaissance deep into enemy territory, the bombing of the Akwal and Gujarat airfields and enemy troops concentrations in the Gujarat and Chawinda areas. In 1971, he led many missions. Notable among these were two raids conducted on the nights of 5 and 7 December 1971 on the Mianwali airfield. He also carried out rocket and four-gun attacks on railway marshalling yards in the Montgomery–Raiwind area with considerable success.

**Q25. The Congo ops were part of the UN mission that was brought about by the breaking away of the state of**

**Katanga from Congo. The IAF mission was to destroy the Katangese Air Force. No. 5 Squadron was based at Leopoldville in huge villas. The airfield had a 5100-yard runway, the longest in the world at that time. Training was carried out here but operations were staged mostly at Kamina near Elisabethville, over 1000 km east, and closer to the operational areas in the rebel province of Katanga. What was the specific and almost unbelievable reason why Kamina too had outstanding facilities?**

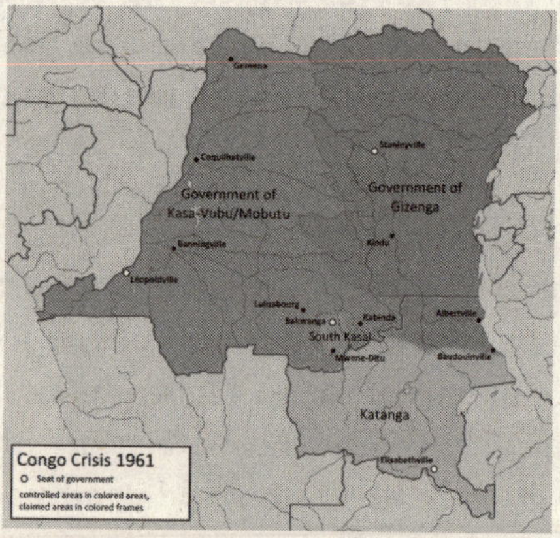


The Congo Crisis map

A25. Kamina had actually been the designated alternative Belgian capital in case of nuclear war in Europe. It was said that its runway surface shone 'like glass'! The base at Kamina was shared with other components of the multinational ONUC force (the United Nations Operation in the Congo—Opération des Nations Unies au Congo, or ONUC), including detachments of Swedish Saab J-29s and Ethiopian F-86 Sabres. The base commander was Swedish, and the base was guarded by a Swedish security battalion.

**Q26. The Katanga province, where the IAF saw its first action on behalf of the United Nations, had been involved in events that had taken place around fifteen to twenty years prior to the UN mission. These events would rank among the top ten of the twentieth century and involved the Shinkolobwe mine in this region. Writing about this mine, an important player, Col Ken Nichols, said: 'Our best source, the Shinkolobwe, represented a freak occurrence in nature. Nothing like it has ever again been found.' What event was this? What was the role of this mine?**

A26. The Manhattan Project. The United States used Shinkolobwe's uranium resources to construct the atomic bomb in World War II. Edgar Sengier, then director of Union Minière du Haut Katanga, had stockpiled 1200 tonnes of uranium ore in a warehouse on Staten Island, New York. This ore and an additional 3000 tonnes of ore stored above-ground at the mine were purchased by Col Ken Nichols for use in the project. The ore already in the US contained 65 per cent U3O8, while the pitchblende above-ground in the Congo amounted to 1000 tons of 65 per cent ore, and the waste piles of ore contained 2000 tons of 20 per cent U3O8. To illustrate the uniqueness of Sengier's stockpile, after the war, the MED and the AEC considered ore containing three-tenths of 1 per cent a good find.

**Q27. In 1947, he was the Secretary of the Army Partition Committee in 1947, which determined the allotment of weapons, equipment and regiments that were to remain in India or to be allotted to Pakistan. Since his parent regiment, the Baluch, went to Pakistan, he was transferred to the Dogra Regiment himself. The second youngest man ever to become a major general, he was the chief of the army staff when the Pokhran nuclear tests took place. Who was this soldier?**

A27. General Gopal Gurunath Bewoor. A seasoned military man, he was also the ambassador to Denmark later. A Padma Bhushan awardee, he has a road named after him in Koregaon Park, Pune. His sons went on to serve in the IAF and served in the Indian Peace Keeping Force (IPKF) campaign. Gen. Bewoor was always a distinguished student who was educated at Colonel Brown Cambridge School, Dehradun, Prince of Wales Royal Indian Military College (RIMC), Dehradun in 1928 and later the Indian Military Academy (IMA). A part of the Kitchener section, Gopal was appointed Cadet Captain in 1934. He also won Lord Rawlinson's trophy during this time.

**Q28. Upon Independence in 1947, India became a dominion within the British Commonwealth of Nations. As a result, the Tudor Crown and four-pointed Bath Star were retained, as George VI remained Commander-in-Chief of the Indian Armed Forces. After 26 January 1950, when India became a republic, the President of India became Commander-in-Chief, and what replaced the Tudor Crown and the Bath Star?**

Evolution of army officer ranks from British to Indian

A28. The Ashoka Lion and the Five-Pointed Star. These were the rank insignias worn by officers. The Ashoka Lion replaced the crown, with a five-pointed star being substituted for the Bath Star.

**Q29. He was born in Amritsar to a doctor who went on to serve as a captain in the British Indian Army with**

**the Indian Medical Service. His younger brother Jami too served in the Indian Armed Forces, becoming a doctor like his father and serving in the Royal Indian Air Force as a medical officer—the first Indian to be awarded the air surgeon's wings from the Naval Air Station Pensacola in the US. Who was this legendary Indian military commander?**

A29. Field Marshal Sam Manekshaw. Manekshaw was selected as part of the first batch of cadets of the IMA called 'The Pioneers'. His class also produced Smith Dun and Muhammad Musa Khan, future commanders-in-chief of Burma and Pakistan, respectively. Training commenced at this academy on 1 October 1932. Manekshaw proved to be very good during his stay at IMA and went on to achieve a number of firsts: the first graduate to join one of the Gorkha regiments; the first to serve as the chief of the army staff of India; and the first to attain the rank of field marshal.

**Did You Know?**

The Lakshadweep Islands were formally included in the dominion of India after an escort of the Travancore Police unfurled the tricolour and beat a Pakistan Navy warship that had set sail from Karachi by only a couple of hours.

**Q30. A pioneer of the IMA, Melville De Mello was from the first batch that graduated from there. He did his schooling at St George's College, Mussoorie, and went on to serve as a lieutenant in the 5/2 Punjab Regiment before joining All India Radio after the end of the Second World War. Known for his baritone voice, he gave commentary for the Republic Day parade for many years as well as for numerous sporting events. He was picked by the British to give radio commentary of the Queen's Coronation procession in 1953 based on his memorable commentary on an event that had taken place a few years prior to that. What was that seminal event?**

A30. Melville De Mello gave a second-by-second commentary on the funeral procession of Mahatma Gandhi. Without a pause, he did a seven-hour continuous commentary, all by himself, hardly able to hold back his own tears. He was the voice of the nation. In recognition of his contribution to broadcasting, he was given the Padma Shri and Padma Bhushan later.

**Q31. A British Indian Army officer and diplomat gives his name to a species of Asian viper and a fish found in the Dasht River in Pakistan. However, his biggest claim to fame is negotiating an agreement in Delhi as part of the 1914 Simla Convention. Who is this, commonly encountered on a map?**

1914 Simla Convention

A31. Henry McMahon, best known for drawing the boundary between Tibet and India (currently the border between India and China) and his correspondence with Hussein bin Ali, the Sharif of Mecca. The 890-km-long line was a result of the Simla Treaty of 1914 between India and Tibet.

**Q32. Edward Abraham Dyer, father of Reginald Dyer—the infamous officer responsible for the Jallianwala Bagh Massacre of 1913—was a Scottish brewer who had established a brewery in Kasauli in 1855 to cater to the British requirement for cheap beer. The brewery transformed into a distillery after he sold a stake in the business to another British entrepreneur H.G. Meakin. After Indian Independence, Narendra Nath Mohan bought a majority stake in the company, which launched an iconic product with a distinct vanilla flavour in 1954 that remains incredibly popular to this day. Which iconic product?**

A32. Old Monk Rum. The famous rum brand comes from the Mohan Meakin Distillery in Kasauli. Before its purchase by Narendra Nath Mohan, it was known as Dyer-Meakin Distillery, named after its founder Edward Abraham Dyer.

**Q33. *Pink and Blue* is a painting by French impressionist Pierre August Renoir that featured two little girls in pink and blue dresses. The girl in the pink dress was named Alice d'Anvers, who later went on to marry Charles Townshend, a British army officer who led the 6th Poona Division in which siege in the Mesopotamian campaign of the First World War?**

A33. The Siege of Kut. In April 1915, Townshend was chosen to command the 6th (Poona) Division in Mesopotamia, tasked with protecting the British Empire's oil production assets in Persia from Ottoman Imperial attack. However, his leadership was greatly called into question after his disastrous defeat at Kut (in modern-day Iraq), in what many call possibly the worst defeat suffered by the Allies.

**Q34. The book *Four Miles to Freedom* by Faith Johnston tells the story of Flt Lt Parulkar and Wg Cdr M.S. Grewal—two IAF pilots who were POWs at a camp in Rawalpindi in the 1971 India-Pakistan War. Inspired by the film *The Great Escape*, and with**

**the help of fellow POW Flt Lt Harish Sinhji, they hatched a plan to escape, using items they managed to source in the camp—such as scissors, forks and an old atlas. After months, they broke through the wall and managed to escape. They boarded a bus for Peshawar, hoping to escape into Afghanistan. Unfortunately, they were caught by locals at a village near Peshawar and brought back to the camp. They were eventually released in December 1972 and given a grand welcome at the Wagah Border. How was their cover blown?**

A34. By asking for directions to a railway station that no longer existed. They were looking for a railway station called 'Landi Khana', which existed during the British times and was shut down after Independence. The atlas given to them at the camp was an old one, so it was marked on that when they were planning to escape. The Landi Khana railway station was located near the town of Torkham, on the Afghan border, and the railway line connecting Landi Khana to the nearby town of Landi Kotal was closed in 1932 at the request of the Afghan government.

**Q35. Thomas Elmhirst was sworn in as the Air Officer Commanding, Royal Indian Air Force, on 15 August 1947 as India became independent. After India became a republic in 1950, his title changed to Commander-in-Chief, Indian Air Force. Apart from leading the air force into the Kashmir War shortly**

**after Independence, what other stately responsibility fell on his shoulders in early 1948 as the then chairman of the chief of staff's committee?**

Mahatma Gandhi's funeral procession

A35. Organizing and supervising the state funeral for Mahatma Gandhi after his death on 30 January 1948. The procession was 8 km long and it took over five hours for the relatively short journey.

**Q36. In the Goan Liberation War of 1961, INS *Betwa* and INS *Beas* fired upon a Portuguese ship at Mormugao Harbour, following which the crew of the ship surrendered to the Indian Navy. The ship, stranded on a beach near Dona Paula, was renamed INS *Saravastri* before being sold for scrap on account of its damage. The ship was originally named after a famous Portuguese explorer who served as the viceroy of Portuguese India from 1509 to 1515, who gives his name to what popular variety of fruit?**

A36. Alphonso mangoes. The famous Alphonso mangoes native to the Konkan region get their name from Afonso de Albuquerque, a Portuguese general, admiral and statesman, and the first Duke of Goa.

**Q37. This astronomical entity was known to the ancient Greeks and was entirely visible as far north as Britain in the fourth millennium BC. However, the precession of the equinoxes gradually lowered them below the European horizon, and they were eventually forgotten by the inhabitants of the northern latitudes. In Hindu mythology, it is said to be a representation of King Trishanku. Where might one be able to spot this astronomical entity in the context of the Indian Army?**

A37. The Southern Cross—the constellation on the emblem of the Southern Command of the Indian Army. A symbol of 'the south', the Southern Cross can also be seen on the flags of several countries south of the equator, most notably on the flags of Australia and New Zealand.

**Q38. Commissioned in 1997, what did the sail training ship INS *Tarangini* do in 2003–04 to create history by becoming the first Indian naval ship to do something?**

A38. Circumnavigated the world. INS *Tarangini* was built not only as a sail training ship but also as an ambassador of India's rich maritime heritage. Keeping this in mind, Cdr H.D. Motiwala, the commissioning captain of the ship, envisioned a plan for travelling around the world in March 2002. The ship was led by Cdr Rahul Mehta on this journey.

**Q39. Completed in August 2022, what was unique about the independent maritime reconnaissance and surveillance mission conducted by the Indian Navy in the North Arabian Sea?**

A39. An all-women crew. This was the first time that such a mission was carried out by a crew made entirely of women, on board a Dornier-228 aircraft. Lt Cdr Aanchal Sharma was the captain of the aircraft and was assisted by Lt Shivangi, Lt Apurva Gite, Lt Pooja Panda and Sub Lt Pooja Shekhawat.

**Q40. Planned to release in 2023, director Aditya Nimbalkar's film *Bull* is set in the backdrop of Operation Cactus, a multi-forces operation by the Indian Armed Forces to thwart a coup d'état in the Maldives against the democratically elected president Gayoom. Played by Shahid Kapoor, who is the protagonist of the film, an Indian Army veteran whose name might remind you of one of the most famous rock stars in history?**

A40. Brig. Farouk Bulsara. He was the commanding officer of the 50th Independent Parachute Brigade, which was airlifted from Agra to Male International Airport in the Maldives on an Ilyushin-76 aircraft. His name might remind you of Freddie Mercury—the lead singer of the famous British rock band Queen—whose birth name was Farrokh Bulsara.

> **Did You Know?**
>
> The prefix 'Surgeon' is used to distinguish naval medical officers from naval officers from other branches irrespective of what speciality they practice.

**Q41. Using Romania, Hungary, Poland and Slovakia as bases, what was the objective of Operation Ganga, conducted by the Indian Army?**

A41. Evacuation of Indian citizens from Ukraine in the midst of the Russian invasion of Ukraine in February 2022.

**Q42. In 1992, the Indian Armed Forces were part of the Unified Task Force (UNITAF), a US-led multinational force of twenty-seven countries assembled to provide a protective environment to conduct humanitarian missions in which African country, torn by civil war?**

A42. Somalia. A United States initiative (codenamed 'Operation Restore Hope'), UNITAF was tasked with creating and maintaining a protected environment, allowing for humanitarian operations in the country.

**Q43. Which future Indian Army chief was awarded the Distinguished Service Order for action during the Battle of Bir Hakiem in Libya during World War II?**

A43. Gen. (then Maj.) P.P. Kumaramangalam. He was born to P. Subbarayan, who served as chief minister of the Madras Presidency between 1926 and 1930. He was taken prisoner of war by the Italians in 1942 but managed to escape in November 1943. Captured again in January 1944 and imprisoned, this time in Germany, he was transferred to Stalag Luft III, a high-security camp for POWs. At the end of the war in 1945, he returned to India. General Kumaramangalam took over as the chief of the army staff on 8 June 1966, the first Indian gunner officer and paratrooper to reach this coveted appointment.

**Q44. During Operation Vijay, conducted in 1961 by the Indian Armed Forces to liberate Portuguese-claimed territories in India, why did K.G. Badlani, an IAS officer, come into the limelight for a day?**

A44. He became the prime minister of Dadra and Nagar Haveli for a day. After Indian Independence in 1947, the residents of Dadra and Nagar Haveli had managed to expel the Portuguese from the colony and enjoyed de facto independence, although this wasn't internationally recognized. To fix this, during Operation Vijay, IAS officer K.G. Badlani was designated the prime minister of the territories of Dadra and Nagar Haveli for one day, so he could sign the instrument of accession which would make these territories a part of the Union of India.

**Q45. Which African country holds the attention on the campus of the National Defence Academy (NDA)?**

A45. Sudan. In 1941, the Government of Sudan sent £1,00,000 as a form of gratitude for the Indian military effort to keep the British colony of Sudan from falling into Italian hands. £70,000 were allotted to India post-Partition and plans were in full swing to create a tri-service academy for cadets of the Indian military. In 1959, the ambassador of Sudan to India, Rahmatullah Abdullah, inaugurated the Sudan Block, the main building of the NDA. The three-storey, basalt and granite structure, with Jodhpur red sandstone, looms large as one enters the 7000-acre campus.

**Q46: What prompted Subroto Mukherjee, 1st CAS, to present the passenger chairs of a particular De Havilland Devon to two future COAS and an army commander, among others?**

A46: These seats were the same in which they had escaped a crash landing by the skin of their teeth. On 3 February 1952, a tactical exercise was planned in Lucknow. Lt Gen. Shrinagesh (future COAS), Maj. Gen. K.S. Thimayya (later COAS), Maj. Gen. S.P.P. Thorat (future GoC-in-C, East), Maj. Gen. Sarda Nand, Maj. Gen. Mohinder Singh Chopra and Brig. Ajaib Singh boarded the flight piloted by Flt Lt Suhas Biswas. On completion, as they departed for Delhi, the port engine caught fire. Flt Lt Biswas put the Devon in a dive to attempt a crash landing before the fuel reserves too caught fire. The turbulence caused the engine mounting to break away.

Flt Lt Biswas finally levelled the airplane and belly-landed successfully at a village near Sandilla. All the general officers walked out without a scratch, with the pilot following them. Each of their seats, along with a plaque, was gifted to them, a memory of the close encounter and the skill of the pilot. Flt Lt Biswas was awarded the Ashok Chakra for having averted a serious crisis in the Indian military leadership.

**Q47: 'Born in Detroit, died in Bhikhiwind,' read Sarvepalli Radhakrishnan in 1965. What was given an inimitable obituary by the President of India?**

A47: The Patton tanks of the Pakistan Army of 1965. When Dr Radhakrishnan visited the battlefield of Asal Uttar, he was greeted by a graveyard of Patton tanks.

The Battle of Asal Uttar saw Pakistan lose ninety-seven tanks in total, of which seventy-two were Pattons. Company Quartermaster Havildar Abdul Hamid had taken out three of the Pattons with his recoil-less gun and was martyred while going for his fourth. He was awarded a posthumous PVC for his bravery. These tanks were then laid out like an open-air showroom, with Pakistan's hopes of winning Amritsar dashed. This also served to dash the so-called superiority of the US's premier Patton tanks, Ayub Khan's racial superiority complex as well as the fact that Pakistan was the premier economy in the region at the time. Thus, Patton Nagar serves as a graveyard for more than just these 'metal elephants'.

**Q48. This is the insignia of which unique equipment of the Indian Navy?**

INS *Jalashwa* badge

A48: This is India's only amphibious transport dock, currently in service! Initially laid down as the USS *Trenton*, she was procured by the Indian Navy in 2005, especially after the 2004 tsunami created a need for a vessel of this calibre. The aptly named vessel is able to carry landing craft, assault amphibious vehicles, landing boats as well as a full retinue of Marine Commandos (MARCOS). Its landing deck opens like the jaws of the hippopotamus, bringing the might of the Indian Navy on to the shore! She saw extensive service during the 2011 Libyan civil war, when she evacuated Indian citizens from the war-torn country, sailing with a full MARCOS crew.

**Q49. The exploits of Capt. (later Brig.) Prashanta Kumar Ghosh form an important part of the history of the Corps of Signals during the operations for the liberation of Bangladesh in 1971. His feat was recognized by the well-deserved award of a Vir Chakra, which he almost missed. Why did Capt. P.K. Ghosh almost miss his award?**

A49. Capt. P.K. Ghosh almost missed the award due to a misunderstanding about his parent formation during the war. It wasn't clear whether he fought the war under 95 MB or from FJ Sector.

**Q50. Contrary to popular belief, Ghosh was not para-dropped with a signal detachment into East Pakistan**

**during the Bangladesh Liberation War in 1971. How did he actually reach East Pakistan? What was his code name?**

A50. Capt. P.K. Ghosh crossed the border on foot with the help of a fourteen-year-old Mukti Bahini trainee code-named Badshah.

**Did You Know?**

In the Battle of Zojila Pass in 1948, the Indian Army did the unthinkable—deploying tanks at 11,553 ft in Ladakh, which was the highest altitude at which tanks were ever deployed till then.

**Q51. Who are known as the 'Phantoms of Chittagong'? How did they earn the nickname?**

A51: The Special Frontier Force, due to their role in guerrilla operations in Chittagong Hill to cut off the retreat route of the Pakistani troops during the Bangladesh Liberation War in 1971. The SFF was also instrumental in training the Mukti Bahini in conjunction with RAW. Indira Gandhi was famously able to rouse them into preventing a genocide of the Bengalis, like the one faced by the Tibetans at the hands of the Communist forces.

**Q52. The Communist Party of China came to power in 1949. Its leader Mao Zedong announced, 'Tibet is**

**the palm that we shall occupy and then go after the five fingers.' What were the five fingers he referred to?**

A52: Ladakh, Nepal, Bhutan, Sikkim and Arunachal Pradesh. This expansionist policy of the People's Republic of China saw them take Aksai Chin in 1962 as it gave the Tibet–Xinjiang highway strategic depth. The People's Liberation Army engages and negotiates with the Indian Army, trying to strong-arm India into keeping its resources occupied on some of the highest battlefields in the world.

**Q53. Robert Tor Russell CIE DSO (1888–1972) was a British architect who was responsible for the development of New Delhi in the early 1930s. He designed the iconic Connaught Place and also served in the First World War in Mesopotamia (Iraq) with the Artists Rifles. What was his architectural contribution to an institution of the Indian Army?**

A53. He designed the Chetwode Hall or the main building of the IMA at Dehradun. He was mentioned in dispatches and awarded the Distinguished Service Order for action during the British advance on Turkish-held Baghdad in the early months of 1917.

**Q54. In 1934, before the first batch had passed out of the IMA, Viceroy Lord Willingdon presented the first**

**colours to the academy on behalf of King George V. The first batch of cadets to graduate from the academy in December 1934 is now known as the Pioneers and included Field Marshal Sam Manekshaw, General Muhammad Musa and General Smith Dun. Which high post did General Smith Dun go on to occupy in future?**

A54. Chief of Army Staff of Burma. General Dun, who was a Kachin, graduated at the top of his class at IMA and also commanded the passing-out parade for the first course. The second, third, fourth and fifth batches were called, respectively, Immortals, Invincibles, Stalwarts and Bahadurs.

**Q55. Seven officers training schools (OTS) were established in India between 1942 and 1945 to meet the huge demand for officers to serve in the Indian and Commonwealth Armies during World War II. They were shut down after the war. In 1962, following the Sino-Indian War, two OTS were established to train officers for emergency commission. The process of establishing the schools was begun in September 1962. One of these was in Chennai. Where was the second one?**

A55. Pune. The Chennai school was inaugurated on 15 January 1963 with Brig. Ram Singh as its first commandant. The Pune school had a short run and was closed in 1964. The school in Chennai continued and in 1965, was converted into a school for training officers for short-service regular commission. OTA Chennai is spread over 750 acres (3 sq. km). Cadets are organized into two battalions, namely Ranjith Singh Battalion and Shivaji Battalion. RS Battalion consists of three companies—Kohima, Jessami and Phillora—and Shivaji Battalion consists of three companies—Meiktila, Naushera and Zojila.

**Q56. Started in Jalandhar in 1925 with donations from the King George V Patriotic Fund, this institution moved to its current location in 1960. Others of its kind are found in Ajmer, Belgaum, Bengaluru and Dholpur. Its alumni have gone on to win the Param Vir Chakra and numerous other awards. Which institution is this?**

A56. Chail Military School or the Rashtriya Military School Chail. Established after the First World War to Indianize the British colonial military in India, it aimed to provide education to young boys with a view to preparing a potential pool of military officers for the future. At present, approximately 300 students from classes six to twelve study here. Capt. G.S. Salaria, who was awarded the PVC for his actions in Katanga, the Congo, studied in this school.

**Q57. Dholpur Military School was established in 1962 by V.K. Krishna Menon. Housed in Kesarbagh Palace, the former ruler's mansion, it has nearly 350 students. Among its alumni is included the youngest person to hold the office of chief minister of Uttar Pradesh. Who is this?**

A57. Akhilesh Yadav. He studied in this school from 1983 to 1990. It is the youngest of the five military schools that are functioning today.

**Q58. Which military institution links the following individuals: Arun Sarin, the former CEO of Vodafone, Navin Nischol, the Bollywood actor who became the first gold medallist of FTII to make it big and Dino Morea, another actor with an Italian father and a mother from Kerala? As is obvious, none of them ever served in the military.**

A58. Bangalore Military School.

**Q59. Tracing its origins back to 1712 with the establishment of a factory by the Dutch Ostend Company, this organization was corporatized and made defunct on 1 October 2021. With revenues of over $3 billion and nearly 80,000 employees, it was the second largest of its category in Asia. Which organization is**

**this, which sold products with names like Nirbheek, Ashani and Prashant, to name a few?**

A59. Ordnance Factory Board. It had forty-one independent factories which have now been merged into seven defence PSUs. The enterprise started in 1712 at Ichchapore, producing gunpowder for the Dutch troops.

**Q60. In the 1980s, fifteen crude oil tankers of the Shipping Corporation of India were named after an elite group. What was common to this group? There are more than fifteen in this group today, but one of those fifteen was unique in that something separated it from the others. What was that?**

A60. PVC winners. The unique one was the tanker named after Flying Officer Nirmal Jit Singh Sekhon of the Indian Air Force—all others were named after winners of the PVC from the Indian Army.

**Did You Know?**

The BSF operates a Quick Reaction Force on the Sir Creek and Indus estuaries called Creek Crocodile Commandos.

**Q61. This company originated from a hammer mill founded in 1646. It started making steel in the 1870s.**

**The company was briefly owned by a tycoon who was mostly responsible for converting it from a steel producer to a participant in the chemical industry and the maker of cannons. It came into national prominence due to its product named Falthaubits 77. Which company was this?**

A61. Bofors. The tycoon was Alfred Nobel, who went on to establish the eponymous set of prizes. Falthaubits 77 is better known in India as the Bofors Gun.

**Q62. The Rod of Asclepius—a staff with a serpent intertwined—is a universal symbol of medicine and healthcare, and can be seen on the insignia of the Indian Army Medical Corps. The Rod of Asclepius is often confused with the caduceus (a staff with two serpents intertwined), which is often used erroneously in place of the Rod of Asclepius. Being a traditional symbol of trade and commerce and held by the Greek figure Hermes, on the logo of which corps of the Indian Army can it be found?**

A62. Corps of Signals. The advent of the telegraph was a major evolutionary step in signalling and had an effect on the Army Signals too. The earliest record of army telegraphy dates back to 1868, when telegraph routes were built by the Army Signals. Till then, signals was one of the functions of the sappers and miners. However, the increased sophistication and enhanced responsibilities saw the birth of the Corps of Signals as a separate arm. It was formed on 15 February 1911, when the 31st and 32nd Divisional Signal Companies, the first Signals units, were raised at Fatehgarh in present-day Uttar Pradesh.

**Q63. A shako is a tall, cylindrical military cap of Hungarian origin, usually adorned with an ornamental badge. Which group within the Indian Army wears blue shakos as part of its ceremonial uniform, which can be traced to the 1843 Battle of Meanee in Sindh?**

Madras Sappers hat

Madras Sappers today

A63. The Madras Sappers. They were the only regiment of the Madras Presidency Army to survive unscathed the extensive reorganizations that took place between 1862 and 1928. The *thambis*, as the troops of the Madras Sappers are popularly known, with their hallmark shakos, have distinguished themselves in many battlefields around the world for more than 200 years. The Bangalore torpedo, a mine-clearing explosive device, was invented in the centre at Bengaluru in the early years of the twentieth century.

**Q64. This weapon, developed by Capt. R.L. McClintock while attached to the Madras Sappers, was used extensively in both world wars, including by the US Army at the D-Day Landings. It is also heavily referenced in the Oscar-winning 1998 film *Saving Private Ryan*, with Capt. Miller (played by Tom Hanks) shouting, 'Bring out the __________!' Which Indian city is this torpedo named after?**

Bangalore torpedo

A64. Bangalore. A Bangalore torpedo is an explosive charge placed within one or several connected tubes.

It is used by combat engineers to clear obstacles that would otherwise require them to approach directly, possibly under fire. It is sometimes colloquially referred to as a 'Bangalore mine', 'banger' or simply 'Bangalore'. Bangalore torpedoes continue to be used today in the little-changed M1A2 and M1A3 versions (United States Armed Forces) and the modified Advanced Performance Bangalore Torpedo version. Newer Bangalore variants include the Alford Technologies Bangalore Blade and the Chemring Advanced Performance Bangalore Torpedo (APBT), with both of these having been developed in the UK.

**Q65. Born into the royal family of Jamnagar, he became the first Indian to be honoured with the Distinguished Service Order during the Second World War for his leadership at Mechili in Libya. In 1955, he briefly became the chief of army staff. Today, several military establishments of a certain kind across the country bear his name, which is what most people would associate him with today. Identify him.**

A65. General Rajendra Sinhji (who gives his name to Rajendra Sinhji Institutes—defence clubs all over India). Gen. Rajendra Sinhji was appointed Commander-in-Chief, Indian Army on 14 January 1953, following the retirement of General (later Field Marshal) K.M. Cariappa.

**Q66. Victor Sassoon was a Jewish businessman who is most notable today for developing the Bund, the central business district of Shanghai, China, in the 1920s. He divided his time between Shanghai and India and owned sprawling properties in Mumbai and Pune. His Pune residence, known as Eves Estate, is home to which establishment today?**

A66. The Army Institute of Physical Training. Eves Estate was also briefly the site of the first campus of the Armed Forces Medical College, Pune, which later moved west to the Connaught Barracks in Wanowrie.

**Q67. Which 1964 Indian film directed by Chetan Anand, starring Balraj Sahni and Dharmendra, depicts a small platoon of Indian soldiers who are considered dead in Ladakh but are rescued by Ladakhi tribesmen and Capt. Bahadur Singh, who dies along with his men trying to hold the Chinese at bay?**

A67. *Haqeeqat*. The film was based on the Battle of Rezang La in Ladakh and showcases a fictionalized version of the last stand of Ahir Company, 13 Kumaon led by Maj. Shaitan Singh. However, the film is not only a representation of war, but a dramatic retelling of the impact war has on the common soldier. Chetan Anand dedicated the film to Jawaharlal Nehru and the soldiers in Ladakh. The film is widely considered one of India's greatest black-and-white war films.

**Q68. James Outram was a British general who made a name for himself in India fighting in the First Anglo-Afghan War and the 1857 war of independence, and was nicknamed the 'Bayard of India'. Which 1977 Satyajit Ray film featured British actor Richard Attenborough playing his role?**

A68. *Shatranj Ke Khiladi*. The Outram Ghat in Kolkata, West Bengal, India, has been named after General Outram, as also Outram Lines, Kingsway Camp, Delhi, India.

**Q69. Which lyricist and singer, famous for being a lyricist for many songs in movies such as *Bobby*, *Amar Prem*, *Sholay*, *Dilwale Dulhania Le Jayenge*, *Pardes* and *Taal*, worked for many years in both the Royal Indian Navy and the independent Indian Army before moving to a career in films?**

A69. Anand Bakshi. He went on to work as a lyricist of over 4000 songs and 638 films in his career and was widely associated with music composers such as Laxmikant–Pyarelal, R.D. Burman, Kalyanji–Anandji, S.D. Burman, Anu Malik, Rajesh Roshan and Anand–Milind. His songs have been sung by all the top singers, including notable ones such as Shamshad Begum, Ila

Arun, Khursheed Bawra, Amirbai Karnataki and Sudha Malhotra. He is known to have worked with more than one generation of music composers. He wrote the first recorded songs of many first-time male and female leads who went on to become stars, and also of singers such as Shailendra Singh, Kumar Sanu, Kavita Krishnamurthy, etc., and he established himself as a versatile lyricist with the song 'Dum Maro Dum' in the movie *Hare Rama Hare Krishna* (1972).

**Q70. Which Indian music director, who won the 1971 National Film Award for Best Music Direction for the soundtrack of the film *Dastak*, joined the Royal Indian Army in 1943 and served for two years till the end of the Second World War, before moving to Mumbai to pursue his musical interests?**

A70. Madan Mohan. He scored the music for *Haqeeqat*. In this, he used Rafi, who sang numbers like 'Kar Chale Hum Fida'. The same film saw Rafi, Talat, Manna Dey and Bhupendra singing 'Hoke Majboor Mujhe Usne Bhulaya Hoga'. Bhupendra appeared on the screen as well for the first time, much before he established himself as a playback singer. This song is also the only song in which four top-rated male playback singers have sung together.

**Did You Know?**

Indian forces were just 1 km from Lahore in 1965 after winning the Battle of Dograi where, against insurmountable odds, an Irish officer led the 3 Jat regiment to victory. None other than famous painter M.F. Hussain was tasked by President Zakir Hussain to cover this and his sketches of Lt Col Desmond Hayde (CO of 3 Jat) remains a rare treasure.

**Q71. When the soil was dredged out during the deepening of the Vembanad lake in 1936, the longest lake in India, it was used to create something that was the largest artificial example of its type. What was created?**

A71. Willingdon Island, the largest artificial island in India, home to the Southern Naval Command.

**Q72. In January 2017, the Indian Navy sent out a press release titled 'India's Largest Bank Teams up with the Nation's Largest Warship'. What was this teaming up all about and why was it unique?**

A72. State Bank of India, India's largest bank, had installed the first ATM aboard a naval vessel in India, on board INS *Vikramaditya*, India's largest ship.

**Q73. In the Indian Navy, whenever a task is done in a group, the count goes 'One, two, six' instead of the usual 'One, two, three'. What's the origin of this practice?**

A73. It is widely believed to derive from the orders used in firing shipboard cannons in the British Royal Navy. According to this story, the team of six gunners had numbered roles. After loading, it was the task of the men numbered two and six to heave (in a coordinated fashion) the cannon out to the gunport for firing, using simple effort for a light cannon or a tackle apiece for larger ones.

The 'two, six, heave' part was picked up by sailors to coordinate seamen's sailing. As used by sailors, the person at the front of the team will typically call out the 'two, six' part of the chant. During this phase, all members move their hands up the line, ready to pull. This is followed, in its natural rhythm, by the 'heave', called out by the whole team together. At this moment, the team simultaneously leans back on the line and uses their leg muscles to exert a powerful pull upon it. Sometime down the line, it got diluted to 'One, two, six' over the ages, although the British *Book of Admiralty* quotes it as early as 1951.

**Q74. In olden times, all messages between ships were exchanged using flags: semaphore. Since the eyesight**

**of an admiral would invariably deteriorate with age, he would need help in comprehending the flag, a source of confusion. What practical solution did the navies of yore come up with, a tradition that still exists?**

The Beatles' *Help!* album cover

A74. He was provided with a lieutenant, a young officer with good eyesight, who would read the signals and convey them to the admiral. This designation, called Flag Lieutenant, persists in multiple naval forces around the world. Interestingly, the Beatles, in their album cover for Help! used semaphore too; however, the positions seemed unappealing for an album cover and their hand positions were changed to 'NUJV' or 'NVUJ' depending on which side of Atlantic the cover was released in.

**Q75. All sailors in the Royal Navy were expected to make their own trousers. To keep things simple, they did not bother to shape the fabric to fit. Instead, they just used it as it came. As the standard width of a bolt of fabric was 54 inches, a sailor just cut it down the middle. After stitching the seams, they were left with two legs with 25 inches around the bottom which became the standard uniform. As it happened, the additional width made it easier to roll them up and keep them clear of water on the deck. What did this eventually give rise to?**

A75. Bell bottoms. This type of trousers was used by British and US naval personnel as well. Originally, these bell bottoms were often just wide-legged trousers and continued to be in use as part of what was called the 'square rig' uniform till as late as 1977.

**Q76. The Anjadiv island, which was the first Indian territory to be occupied by the Portuguese in 1502, four years after the arrival of Vasco da Gama and eight years before the conquest of Goa, was also the last to be surrendered as it was liberated only on 22 December 1961, two days after Goa. Which anomaly does it represent, caused by the Goan government's decision to hand it over to the Indian Navy in 1991?**

A76. Even though the closest shore is Karwar in Karnataka, now connected to the Karnataka mainland by a breakwater, revenue-wise, the island is under the jurisdiction of the South Goa collector and is still a part of Goa.

**Q77. In the 1600s, seafaring being a huge part of global trade, sailors had to navigate the deep blue seas to sell merchandise and trade goods. Sailors who went on these journeys had to caulk or protect the seams, a part of the hull of their vessels that was closest to the water. If they didn't, their ships would be torn apart. This problem was also complicated because it was easy for a sailor to die while performing this task. What name was given to these seams in common parlance, known to us in a different context?**

A77. Devils. Hence the idiom 'between the devil and the deep blue sea'.

**Q78. In *fauji* messes around the world, table etiquette demands that hands/elbows never be put on the table while eating. However, an exception to this rule exists. A mariner who's sailed to two specific places of great importance in naval history is allowed to place his hands/elbows on the table (in medieval times, he was allowed to place his legs too). Which two places we'd all have encountered during high-school geography mapping classes are being spoken of?**

A78. The Cape of Good Hope and Cape Horn.

**Q79. The French fighter aircraft Ouragan was the first-ever aircraft acquired by India that was given an Indian name. It was called Toofani—a literal translation of ouragan/hurricane. The real impetus to renaming came when MiG 23/27s were being acquired in the early 1980s, in order to avoid confusion between different types of MiG aircraft. Who selected the Indian names for the aircraft in the IAF?**

A79. Air Chief Marshal Dilbagh Singh. He was given a long list of names from which he selected the Indian names for the aircraft. The HAL-produced aircraft always had an Indian name—and continue to do so even today—Tejas and Dhruv being examples. However, due to trouble with foreign vendors being unable to pronounce Indian names, the practice of giving local names to imported aircraft is currently suspended. Hence, Su-30s, Embraer, Do-228s and Rafales do not have Indian names.

**Q80. This pair of twin cities, one in India and the other in Pakistan, both have names that mean 'mound of the dead' in Gujarati and Sindhi. While the Indian city houses the oldest 'dock' in the world, the Pakistani city derives its fame from being the largest city in the Indus Valley civilization. Name these cities.**

A80. While Lothal, near the current city of Ahmedabad, served as the port to the Indus Valley civilization, Mohenjo Daro in Larkana, Sindh, Pakistan, was rediscovered in 1919 by Rakhal Das Banerji.

**Q81. The largest contemporary art festival in Asia takes its name from two cities, both of immense importance in the naval history of India. While one is a modern-day metropolis, the other is its mythical predecessor. Which is the art festival being spoken of?**

A81. Kochi-Muziris Art Biennale. The port town of Muziris, situated near modern-day Kodungallur served to export spices such as black pepper, ivory and precious stones into Arabia and Europe of antiquity.

**Q82. The wardroom of INHS *Asvini*, the flagship tertiary care naval hospital in Mumbai, has a nickname given to it because of the large gusts of wind it receives due to its huge windows. What name is this, which might remind many of a 'palace' in another part of India?**

A82. Hawa Mahal. The gusts of winds received are reminiscent of the Hawa Mahal of Jaipur, both literally and figuratively.

**Q83. Karwar, a nondescript coastal town in Uttara Kannada, Karnataka, also home to INS *Vikramaditya***

**and the largest naval base in Asia, has a lot of restaurants, establishments and even private bus and transport services strangely named after a particular bird. Which bird, and what's the connection?**

A83. Seabird. Named after Project Seabird, the parent project which led to the creation of the naval base in Karwar.

**Q84. The Indian Navy names a lot of its establishments with careful thought after cities, mythological places, rivers and weapons. One of the transit accommodation buildings for officers in Kochi takes its name from _____, a place where the Pandavas stayed for a short period while in exile. Which place?**

A84. Ekachakra, a place in the present-day Birbhum district of West Bengal. Legend has it that during the Battle of Kurukshetra, the closest that Lord Krishna came to breaking his vow of not participating in the war was when he picked up a wheel in anger and came charging towards Bhishma, who was fighting Arjuna. Seeing this, Bhishma started singing praises of Krishna. This dissipated his anger and he threw away the wheel, which landed at the site of modern-day Ekachakra ('singular wheel').

**Q85. One of India's oldest and largest business conglomerates, with a presence across chemicals,**

**engineering services, lamination, precision springs, real estate, aviation and sport, was founded in 1736 when its founder set up a marine construction company, one of India's earliest, which went on to build 355 ships, including the first ships constructed for the British Navy outside England. Which business group is this?**

A85. The Wadia group. One might see their crest while boarding a GoFirst flight. They are also the conglomerate behind the ubiquitous Britannia and Bombay Dyeing.

**Q86. In 1971, INS *Rajput*, an Indian Navy destroyer, set out from Vizag Port with specific instructions to mimic the appearance and wireless traffic of another ship. Which ship was INS *Rajput* instructed to impersonate and what was the consequence of that?**

A86. It was supposed to mimic INS *Vikrant*, India's only aircraft carrier back then. PNS *Ghazi* got lured in and was sunk by the depth charges launched by INS *Rajput* as a consequence.

**Q87. The 'crossing the line' ceremony is an age-old custom celebrated across navies whenever someone who's never crossed the equator makes it to the other side. The initiation ritual involves presenting the individual in Lord Neptune's court, usually a sailor masquerading as the sea god, and being asked to do**

**fun tasks like tasting/taking a dip in seawater. The Indian Navy also has a similar ceremony presided over by Lord _____. Whose court would one be appearing in if one was to cross the equator as part of the Indian Navy? Fill in the blank.**

A87. Lord Varuna.

**Q88. Located on India's east coast, this beach is unique in the sense that the sea recedes by almost 2–3 km during high and low tides, not only enthralling visitors with its 'disappearing act' but also allowing them to literally walk into the sea during these phases. More famous for being home to the DRDO's Integrated Testing Range, which has tested missiles like Agni, Aakash and Prithvi, name this beach town.**

A88. Chandipur.

**Q89. British company Martin Baker and its French partner Safran Martin Baker are the premium manufacturers of this product worldwide and command 56 per cent market share across the world. Their clients for this product include the armed forces of multiple nations, including the Indian Navy and the Indian Air Force. It also runs an exclusive club with a lifetime membership for clients who manage to use their products 'successfully', a number estimated to be a little over 5000 worldwide. Which product does**

**Martin Baker make? What exclusive club is being referred to?**

A89. Ejection seats from fighter jets and the Ejection Tie Club for pilots who have successfully managed to eject from crashing jets.

**Q90. This term was first used to mean 'having the highest qualifications' in reference to commercial ships. The term referred to the highest possible rating in the system instituted prior to 1800 by the famous insurer Lloyd's of London. Lloyd's registry of ships explains this rating thus: 'The first character denotes new ships or ships renewed or restored. The storage condition of vessels is designated by the second character.' Since shipping was of such great importance to the British economy in the eighteenth and nineteenth centuries and since Lloyd's was so well known, the rating system became a part of the public lingo and was soon used to express one's admiration for a vessel by referring to it as an '_____ ship'. What is being spoken of here?**

A90. How A1 started to mean 'of the highest quality'.

**Q91. Built at a cost of Rs 23,000 crore, with steel equivalent to three Eiffel Towers and a speculated power generation capacity enough to light up 'half of Kochi city', it goes by the motto '*Jayema Sam Yudhi***

***Sprudhah*' from the Rigveda, which means 'I conquer those who fight me'. What is being spoken of?**

A91. India's latest aircraft carrier, INS *Vikrant*.

**Q92. Initially the Pacific Coast Hindustan Association, it was formed in 1913 in the US under the leadership of Baba Sohan Singh Bhakna as its president. It drew members from Indian immigrants, largely from Punjab. Many of its members were also from the University of California at Berkeley, including Dayal, Tarak Nath Das, Kartar Singh Sarabha and V.G. Pingle. The party quickly gained support from Indian expatriates, especially in the US, Canada and Asia. Meetings were held in Los Angeles, Oxford, Vienna, Washington, DC and Shanghai. The ultimate goal was to overthrow British colonial authority in India by means of an armed revolution with a strategy to entice Indian soldiers to revolt. To that end, in November 1913, it established the Yugantar Ashram Press in San Francisco. Which entity are we talking about here?**

A92. The Ghadar Party. The Ghadar Mutiny, also known as the Ghadar Conspiracy, started at the onset of World War I, between the Ghadar Party in the US, the Berlin Committee in Germany, the Indian revolutionary underground in British India and the German Foreign Office through the consulate in San

Francisco. Indian units as far as Singapore were poised to participate in the rebellion. The plans were thwarted through a coordinated intelligence and police response. British intelligence infiltrated the Ghadarite movement in Canada and in India, and last-minute intelligence from a spy helped crush the planned uprising in Punjab before it started. Key figures were arrested, and mutinies in smaller units and garrisons within India were also crushed. The conspiracy was followed by the First Lahore Conspiracy Trial and Benares Conspiracy Trial, which saw death sentences awarded to a number of Indian revolutionaries and the exile of a number of others. After the end of the war, fear of a second Ghadarite uprising led to the passage of the Rowlatt Act, followed by the Jallianwala Bagh massacre.

**Q93. One of the oldest Indian Army units, Assam Rifles (AR) started as Cachar Levy (named after the Cachar Hills) in 1835 to protect British tea gardens from tribal raids. Since its origin, it has often been called the 'right arm of the civil and left arm of the military', a fact which is reflected in its unique C2 (command and control structure). What is this unique C2?**

A93. The only force to have a dual command, that is, administrative control exercised by the Ministry of Home Affairs (MHA) and operational control by the

Indian Army. Interestingly, till 1965, AR was under the overall control of the MEA (foreign ministry), since the territories of the North-Eastern Frontier Agency (NEFA), which form modern-day Arunachal, Mizoram and parts of Assam, were administered by an MEA political resident until transfer to the MHA in 1965. Thus, AR has functioned under the MEA, MHA as well as the Army.

**Q94. In the late 1950s, posted in the desolate Lumla Post of NEFA, an Assam Rifles platoon received a top-secret order from the PMO to immediately proceed to outpost Shakti on foot and escort a secretive retinue of twenty. In a fateful demonstration of Indian 'shakti', who was this AR platoon escorting?**

Dalai Lama with Havildar Das in 2017 in Guwahati

A94. The Dalai Lama. Out of the original seven members of the 9th Platoon, two died in the 1962 war. The sole survivor, Havildar Naren Chandra Das, joined the Dalai Lama in an emotional reunion in 2017 in Guwahati. The Dalai Lama, his closest family and ministers fled Lhasa in March 1959. Interestingly, it is said the detailed escape route was revealed to the Dalai Lama by his personal oracle and he was able to evade the PLA in Lhasa by disguising himself in a Chinese military uniform. He was escorted by Mustang division, a Great Game-era military force set up with CIA support.

**Q95. Ralengnao 'Bob' Khathing was a renowned diplomat and administrator, becoming the first person of tribal origin to be an Indian ambassador. In 1950, Khathing became known for leading a daring operation of 200 Assam Rifles soldiers that led to a peaceful transfer of power in a strategic, holy border town that would later be used by the Dalai Lama to enter India. Which town is this, known for its famous monastery?**

A95. Tawang. Until 1950, Tawang was under Tibetan administrative control. Realizing the strategic importance of Tawang in a future Indo-China conflict, Khathing arrived in the town with 200 soldiers and 600 porters in 1950. Taking advantage of a local tax grievance against Tibetan authorities by the local Monpa tribe, Khathing used his diplomatic tact to convince the local populace to cede to India, thus leading to a peaceful transfer of power. Khathing would later be instrumental in the setting up of the Sashastra Seema Bal (SSB) after the 1962 war debacle to guard parts of Nepal and the Bhutan border.

**Q96. The Assam Rifles have been instrumental as a counter-insurgency force. Along with the Malabar Special Police (MSP), they played a key role in subduing a controversial revolt against British rule that eventually turned into an ethnic massacre in 1921–22. What is this infamous revolt, named after a particular type of Malabari sword, and might also remind one of a North Kerala cuisine?**

A96. The Moplah Rebellion. Moplah cuisine from North Kerala has a unique flavour, blending Arabic, Persian, Indian and European styles with the emblematic dish, Thalassery Biryani. MSP was set up as a counter-riots and insurgency force to tackle Alluri Sitaram Raju's guerrilla forces. Remnants of it still exist in Tamil Nadu and Kerala State Police.

**Q97. An Assam Rifles unit in 2020, led by an ASC officer, Maj. Gursimran Kaur, made history in the icy mountains of Sadhna Top. A historic first was achieved that necessitated a modification of a common rank to be made more inclusive of modern changes. What change? What historic first?**

Evolution of the Assam Rifles emblem

A97. It was the first time women were being deployed in front-line combat roles in the LOC. The change in rank was from 'Rifleman' to 'Riflewoman'.

**Q98. The Assam Rifles regimental badge has seven distinctive black rays to showcase its chief area of operations. What do these seven rays signify?**

Assam Rifles badge

A98. These represent the 'Seven Sisters', aka the north-eastern states, where AR is most active. The term 'seven sisters' was first used to describe the seven north-eastern states by Jyoti Prasad Saikia in 1972.

**Q99. The idea of a unified Air Force Academy (AFA) for flying and ground duty branches (except technical) was born in IAF senior command in 1953. Eventually, an ideal site, equidistant from Hyderabad and Secunderabad, was chosen as the weather was conducive for flying training, and the satellite bases of Hakimpet and Bidar were nearby for advanced training. Which is this city on which the modern-day AFA stands, often confused with a historic Tamil city?**

A99. Dundigal, not to be confused with Dindigul, which is a town in Tamil Nadu. The technical branch specialization is done in Air Force Technical College (AFTC) at Jalahalli, Bangalore.

**Q100. The AFA, being a sensitive installation, has rarely granted permission as a shooting location. An exception was made for a 1982 war film directed by Govind Nihalani that was highly commended for its realistic portrayal of the IAF, including the novel use of real IAF MiG 21 Bison engaged in aerial battles, due to which it has been called the 'Indian Top Gun'.**

**Which Shashi Kapoor film was this, starring him along with his son?**

*Vijeta* film poster

A100. *Vijeta*. The movie was made to coincide with the golden jubilee of the IAF in 1982 and was shot on location at a number of sensitive IAF bases. It was the debut of Shafi Inamdar, who would later gain fame in *Ardh Satya*, Kundan Shah's *Yeh Jo Hai Zindagi* and *Krantiveer*. Inamdar tragically died of a heart attack after watching India lose in the 1996 ICC Cricket World Cup semis.

**Q101. Established in 1969 and operationalized in 1971, the AFA had as its first commandant a pilot whose name might remind you of a hearty pioneer of Philippine democracy. Who was this?**

A101. Air Cmde J.D. Aquino. Corazon Aquino ended the dictatorship of Marcos in the Philippines as leader of the People Power Revolution and became her country's first female head of state.

**Q102. Which seminal, progressive decision was taken by the AFA as per the SC decision of 1992 along with the Indian Army for the batch of 1993?**

A102. The induction of lady cadets into the AFA. The first lady cadet to be commissioned into the Indian Army via OTA Chennai in 1993 along with other twenty-four trailblazers was Priya Jhinghan. Before 1993, women could be commissioned only via the medical branch, that is, the Army Medical Corps (AMC) or Military Nursing Service (MNS). Similarly, in the IAF, women were commissioned as cadets via AFA for the first time in 1993, before which only medical roles were accepted. INA Ezhimala (Indian Naval Academy) has been accepting lady cadets since its inception while NDA will welcome its first batch of lady cadets in 2023.

**Q103. Air Chief Marshal L.M. Katre was the Chief of Air Staff (CAS) from 1984–85. The only AFA commandant to eventually rise to the apex position of CAS, he's known for expanding the ground training branch in the AFA. Which tragic record does he hold in the annals of IAF history?**

A103. He is one of the only two CAS to die in harness along with First CAS ACM Subroto Mukherjee.

**Q104. One of the seven Central Armed Police Forces (CAPF) organizations, raised as a consequence of the 1962 war to protect the contentious Tibet border, has over the years transformed into a key disaster response force trained in NBC (nuclear, biological and chemical warfare), with two units deployed to the National Disaster Response Force (NDRF). Identify this force, known as the 'Sentinel of the Himalayas'.**

A104. The Indo-Tibetan Border Police (ITBP). It is governed by the ITBP Act 1992 as of 1996 and functions as one of the seven CAPF (commonly called paramilitary forces) under the MHA. The other six are CRPF, CISF, BSF, SSB (Sashastra Seema Bal, which protects Nepal and the Bhutan border), Assam Rifles and NSG (National Security Guard, popularly called the Black Cats, specialized in VVIP protection and counter-terror ops).

**Q105. ITBP personnel are specialists in high-altitude warfare, protecting a 3488 km-long border from the Karakoram Pass in Ladakh to Diphu Pass in Arunachal. Their bravery in the most difficult of snowy terrains has led them to be referred to with a two-worded moniker. What is this moniker, true to their motto of '*Shaurya, Dridhata, Karm, Nishtha*'?**

A105. Him veer. *Him* means 'snow' and *veer* means 'brave' in Hindi. The M&SI (Mountaineering and Skiing Institute) was set up in Auli (near Joshimath) in 1973–74 to train ITBP cadres in high-altitude warfare, mountaineering and winter sports. In 2022, ITBP opened its second high-altitude warfare institute in remote Dombang in Sikkim, especially to train in countering PLA intrusions in the region. The High Altitude Warfare School (HAWS) of the Indian Army was founded in 1948 in Gulmarg, Jammu and Kashmir. Open to friendly militaries and routinely visited by American, British and German soldiers, it's India's most elite high-altitude warfare school, with advanced courses on mountain warfare and winter warfare, with a special ice craft course taught at Machoi in the heights of Zojila.

**Q106. ITBP has a unique veterinary unit which is trained in handling and management of a particular asset key to transportation and logistics in high-altitude regions. Undergoing specialized training for it in the ICAR National Research Institute, what is this key Tibetan asset?**

A106. Yaks. Yak racing and yak polo are popular sports in Tibet, Nepal and Gilgit Baltistan. Yaks or Bos grunniens are also known as Tartary Ox. The scientific name of the domestic yak means grunting bull, while the wild variety is named Bos mutus or silent bull. It was named so by Russian geographer and explorer Nikolay Przhevalsky, who believed erroneously that it makes no sound at all.

**Q107. In a formal *namkaran* (naming) ceremony in Bhanu, Panchkula, in a notable shift from traditional names, seventeen Malinois pups were chosen for the K9 unit of the ITBP. Some of these were Ane la, Sasoma, Chip Chap, Saser, Rezang, Chardin, Shyok and one more. What shift in tradition is being talked about here in an attempt to decolonize ITBP legacy? Identify the last puppy's name, a river which has been the site of brutal battles in both 1962 and 2020..**

A107. Giving its K9 unit dogs 'indigenous names' after positions in Ladakh defended by the ITBP. Prior to this, most ITBP dogs were given Russian names like Gala, Olga and Oleshya.

The pup was named Galwan, made popular due to the Chinese intrusion in April–June 2020.

**Q108. In August 2021, a curious petition was filed by thirty ITBP members in the Delhi HC, asking for redeployment to a very dangerous station that led to the HC bench being 'amazed' by the request. Where was the requested station, which was in the news in August 2021 for a risky, massive Indian evacuation?**

A108. Afghanistan. ITBP personnel are specially trained in diplomatic security and were posted to the Indian embassy in Kabul and to consulate generals in Kandahar and Mazar-i-Sharif. The Indian embassy and consulate staff were evacuated from Kabul in an IAF aircraft that included up to ninety-nine ITBP commandos and K9 dogs.

**Q109. In a highly publicized case, Malharrao of Baroda would be found guilty by a British inquiry and deposed for poisoning the British Resident Phayre. Along with the common arsenic, which highly expensive material was said to have been used as an unconventional poison by Malharrao to poison Phayre?**

Malharrao Gaekwad and Resident Phayre of Baroda

A109. Diamond dust. It's said that arsenic and diamond dust were mixed in Phayre's sherbet. Malharrao was deposed in April 1875 on the orders of Secretary of State for India, Lord Salisbury, and died in obscurity in Madras in 1882 while Phayre was removed as Resident too. A new successor was chosen by the British Government, whose real name was Gopalrao. He was given a new name, Sayajirao, and he ascended the throne on 16 June 1875.

**Q110. In the 17th century, Ahom king Pratap Singha established the administrative ministry of 'five *patra mantris*' with Burgohain ruling north and south of the Dikhow river, Borpatrogohain ruling the region from the Defala hills to the Brahmaputra, and Borbarua and another mantri ruling the areas around the Kalibor river. Name this 'mantri', an administrative position familiar to us as the name of a legendary Assamese military general.**

A110. Borphukan.

**Q111. In 1999, Army Chief Gen. V.P. Malik announced the renaming of a coveted award in one of India's most elite academies to honour Lachit Borphukan's military glory. Which is this award?**

Statue of Lachit Borphukan

A111. The Best Overall Cadet award. It is now called the Lachit Borphukan Medal in the NDA and is awarded every year to the 'Best Overall Cadet' from each batch. A statue of Lachit adorns the campus of NDA.

**Q112. Veerta Chakra is the second circle in the National War Memorial plan, which showcases six bronze murals by Ram Sutar depicting the battles of Gangasagar, Tithwal, Rezang La, Trident, and two others. The former was depicted famously in a fictionalized Bollywood portrayal, in which a single Sikh unit stopped a division-level armoured offensive. The latter, named after a Kalidasa work, was the Indian operation to capture the heights of Siachen. Identify both.**

A112. The Battle of Longewala (of *Border* movie fame) and Meghdoot. Ram Sutar, the artist behind the murals, has also sculpted the Vallabhbhai Patel Statue of Unity in Gujarat.

**Q113. The National War Memorial (NWM) construction was designated as a special project and allocated to the Special Projects Division under the chief administrative officer of the MoD and MES. Under it, a global design competition was held that finally chose a Chennai-Coimbatore-based**

**architecture company in 2017 to lead the project. Which company, and who was the lead architect?**

Yogesh Chandrahasan

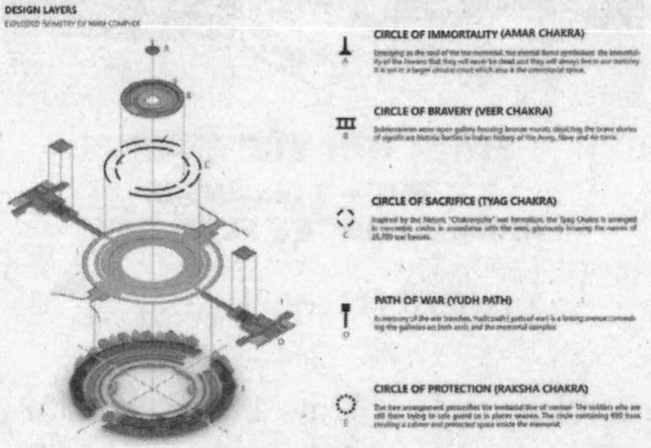


NWM isometric view

A113. Webe Design Lab and Yogesh Chandrahasan. The NWM is built as four concentric circles and a central obelisk, at the bottom of which burns the Amar Jawan Jyoti. This concentric plan is inspired by the *chakravyuh* described in the Mahabharata.

**Q114. As per protocol, seven official events are annually held at the National War Memorial, which includes Republic Day, Army Day, Navy Day, Air Force Day, Kargil Vijay Diwas and Vijay Diwas (16 December, to celebrate the 1971 war victory). The seventh event is a lesser-known occasion celebrated annually on 7 December since 1948, which aims at collecting funds for the rehabilitation of battle casualties and the welfare of former servicemen and their families via a fund of the same name. What is the occasion aptly known as?**

Armed Forces Flag Day

A114. Armed Forces Flag Day. The CDS, along with the three service chiefs, attend this event annually. The flag is similar to the British MOD, with the colour scheme of the fellow Commonwealth nations of Cyprus, Kenya and Nigeria.

**Q115. *The Lovers* is a 2013 Belgian romance time-travel adventure film starring Josh Hartnett and**

**Bipasha Basu, based on a story by Ajey Jhankar, exploring the fictitious romance between Capt. James Stewart and warrior Tulaja Naik. Which war forms the backdrop for the film?**

A115. The First Anglo-Maratha War.

# Image Sources

Page 3, Polar area diagram: https://commons.wikimedia.org/wiki/File:Nightingale-mortality.jpg

Page 13, Saragarhi Memorial, Ferozepur: https://upload.wikimedia.org/wikipedia/commons/c/c7/Saragarhi_Memorial_Ferozepur.jpg

Page 16, Madras Regiment insignia: https://en.wikipedia.org/wiki/Madras_Regiment#/media/File:Madras_Regiment_insignia_(India).svg

Page 17, Grenadiers insignia: https://en.wikipedia.org/wiki/The_Grenadiers#/media/File:Grenadiers_Insignia_(India).svg

Page 24, Scinde Horse badge: https://stampwala.com/product/india-postage-2012-the-scinde-house-first-day-brochure-iib1/

Page 29, Kumaon Regiment insignia: https://en.wikipedia.org/wiki/File:Kumaon_Regiment_Insignia_(India).svg

Page 30, Ludhiana Sikhs badge: https://collection.nam.ac.uk/detail.php?acc=2013-10-20-37-39

Page 31, Coins of Kandahar: https://www.cngcoins.com/Coin.aspx?CoinID=363815

Page 32, MacGregor medal: https://en.wikipedia.org/wiki/MacGregor_Medal#/media/File:MacGregor_Medal.jpg

Page 33, The Battle of the Sittang Bridge: https://z-upload.facebook.com/TheGurkhaMuseum/photos/pcb.4923721677694850/4923721517694866/ ?type=3&theater

Page 34, Hengdang sword: https://www.artstation.com/artwork/03k GOK

Page 36, War Memorial, Noida: https://lbb.in/delhi/war-memorial-noida-golf-course-battle-of-delhi/

Page 37, The Battle of Saraighat map: https://twitter.com/varadadya/status/1410562323819819016

Page 42, Indian soldiers at Gallipoli: https://edtimes.in/indian-soldiers-made-far-more-contribution-to-the-great-war-than-their-own-independence-movement/

Page 45, Royal Pavilion, Brighton: https://en.m.wikipedia.org/wiki/Royal_Pavilion#/media/File:Brighton_royal_pavilion_Qmin.jpg

Page 47, Hardit Singh Malik's Casualty Card: http://www.empirefaithwar.com/tell-their-story/citizen-historians-in-action/soldier-stories-blog/hardit-singh-malik

Page 52, Tulbahadur Pun train: https://www.gwt.org.uk/news/great-western-railway-name-train-in-honour-of-gurkha-soldier-tul-bahadur-pun-vc/

Page 57, Chindits patch: https://www.uswarspatches.com/ww2-oss-3rd-indian-division-bullion-with-tab-patch-c/

Page 58, Battle of Kohima map: https://www.forces-war-records.co.uk/blog/2017/04/21/was-your-ancestor-in-britains-greatest-battle

Page 64, Lt Gen. W.B. Leishman: https://en.wikipedia.org/wiki/William_Boog_Leishman#/media/File:Sir_William_Boog_Leishman._Photomechanical_print_by_after_Ba_Wellcome_V0026696.jpg

Page 65, Number of deaths from kala-azar in Assam: https://commons.wikimedia.org/wiki/File:Number_of_Deaths_from_Kala-Azar_in_Assam.svg

Page 65, Dr Upendranath Brahmachari: https://www.anandranga nathan.com/2017/08/19/686/

Page 67, INA Memorial, Moirang: https://commons.wikimedia.org/wiki/File:INA_Memorial,_Moirang,_Manipur_%2812%29.jpeg

Page 68, The Battle of Tennis Court: https://i.redd.it/2r1m9065f1771.jpg

Page 68, Tennis Court then and now: https://twitter.com/INagaland/status/1411748567593537536/photo/1

Page 69, Rhino hat: https://military-history.fandom.com/wiki/Assam_Regiment?file=IndianArmyDelhi.JPG

Page 70, One-horned rhino: https://www.thestatesman.com/india/kaziranga-population-one-horned-rhinoceros-increases-200-last-4-years-1503055685.html

Page 70, Dah sword: https://rossarms.com/burmese-dah-short-sword

Page 71, Kohima War Memorial: https://commons.m.wikimedia.org/wiki/File:Kohima_War_Memorial_(2).jpg

Page 81, Punjab Regiment insignia: https://en.wikipedia.org/wiki/Punjab_Regiment_%28India%29

Page 88, Tashkent Declaration: https://www.rediff.com/news/special/no-iota-of-doubt-about-shastris-death/20190525.html

Page 98, Tangail Paradrop: https://twitter.com/rajnathsingh/status/1469859501436469248/photo/1

Page 101, Rashtriya Rifles badge: https://bluearmy.co.in/collections/rashtriya-rifles

Page 103, Patka helmet: https://www.armoursteel.in/bullet-proof-patka.html

Page 104, Lance Naik Ahmad Wani: https://twitter.com/love_for_nation/status/1463795877244379137

Page 105, Brig. Sawai Bhawani Singh awarded the Maha Vir Chakra: https://www.tribuneindia.com/news/features/

brigadier-sawai-bhawani-singh-brigadier-sukhjit-singh-the-maha-virs-291298

Page 107, 10 Para in action: https://www.facebook.com/TeamINDRA/photos/pcb.1019733954834955/1019733911501626/ ?type= 3&theater

Page 108, Brig. B.S. Shergill and Col R. Chauhan: https://www.facebook.com/honourpoint/photos/a.231696397307640/934173913726548/?type=3

Page 119, Kurt Tank: https://www.facebook.com/TheSecretHorsepowerRace/photos/a.183947085357262/1227849250967035/?type=3

Page 122, The Engineers: https://i0.wp.com/www.bharat-rakshak.com/IAF/images/history/ww2/engineers/MinooAspyRonnie.jpg

Page 125, Raveena Tandon bomb: https://www.google.com/amp/s/www.opindia.com/2021/07/kargil-vijay-diwas-raveena-tandon-nawaz-sharif-missile/amp/

Page 128, The Congo Crisis map: https://en.wikipedia.org/wiki/Congo_Crisis#/media/File:Kongo_1961_map_en.png

Page 131, Evolution of army officer ranks: https://en.m.wikipedia.org/wiki/File:British_Army_(1920-1953)_OF-5.svg

Page 134, 1914 Simla Convention: https://en.m.wikipedia.org/wiki/Simla_Convention

Page 137, Mahatma Gandhi's funeral procession: https://www.merepix.com/2013/05/mahatma-gandhi-funeral-rare-photos.html?m=1

Page 144, INS *Jalashwa* badge: https://en.m.wikipedia.org/wiki/INS_Jalashwa_(L41)#/media/File%3AINS_Jalashwa_emblem.JPG

Page 153, Madras Sappers hat: https://en.m.wikipedia.org/wiki/Shako

Page 153, Madras Sappers today: https://m.facebook.com/photo.php?fbid=636981507002942&id=137986450235786&set=a.138008500233581&source=48&refid=13&__tn__=%2B%3E

Page 154, Bangalore torpedo: https://www.thequint.com/news/india/a-100-year-old-weapon-called-bangalore-still-use-by-the-us-army

Page 161, The Beatles' *Help!* album cover: https://www.beatle.net/looking-for-help-recollections/

Page 172, Dalai Lama with Havildar Das: https://newsable.asianetnews.com/india-defence/remembering-havildar-naren-chandra-das-who-escorted-dalai-lama-while-he-was-fleeing-r4wx9n

Page 175, Evolution of the Assam Rifles emblem: https://salute.co.in/assam-rifles/

Page 175, Assam Rifles badge: https://salute.co.in/assam-rifles/

Page 177, *Vijeta* film poster: https://www.amazon.in/-/hi/Shashi-Kapoor/dp/B0086UPA92

Page 182, Malharrao Gaekwad and Resident Phayre of Baroda: https://theprint.in/pageturner/excerpt/a-maharajah-in-court-baroda-king-tried-for-poisoning-british-officer/740961/

Page 183, Statue of Lachit Borphukan: https://twitter.com/Voice OfAxom/status/1198455910357585920

Page 185, Yogesh Chandrahasan: https://www.mynation.com/india-news/meet-yogesh-chandrahasan-the-chennai-based-architect-who-designed-national-war-memorial-pnuacp

Page 185, NWM isometric view: https://www.archidiaries.com/projects/circle-of-rebirth_-national-war-memorial-webe-design-lab-chennai/

Page 186, Armed Forces Flag Day: https://www.timesnownews.com/viral/armed-forces-flag-day-2022-wishes-quotes-messages-and-whatsapp-status-to-share-article-96030803